Y0-ABE-004

SACRAMENTO PUBLIC LIBRARY

3 3029 05336 2315

CENTRAL LIBRARY
828 "I" STREET
SACRAMENTO, CA 95814
JAN - - 2004

THE
JELLY
DONUT
DIET
BOOK

THE JELLY DONUT DIET BOOK

Judge Lawrence Grey

M. Evans and Company, Inc.
New York

Copyright © 2003 by Lawrence Grey

All rights reserved. No portion of this book may be reproduced or transmitted in any form or by any means without the written permission of the publisher.

Illustrations by Grover C. McAlister

M. Evans and Company, Inc.
216 East 49th Street
New York, New York 10017

Library of Congress Cataloging-in-Publication Data

Grey, Lawrence.
    The jelly donut diet book / Lawrence Grey.
      p.   cm.
   1. American wit and humor. I. Title.
    PN6165.G74 2003
    818'.607—dc22   2003019777

Book design and typesetting by Rik Lain Schell

Printed in the United States of America

9 8 7 6 5 4 3 2 1

for Aaron, Matthew, Logan, and Anne

Contents

Introduction

American society has had a long tradition of free expression and robust open debate on the important issues of the day. We all believed Milton when he said, "Let Truth and Falsehood grapple; whoever knew Truth to be bested in a free and open encounter?"

Being a judge for over twenty-five years has given me a more tolerant view of the world. A judge's job is sort of like following the parade of life with a broom and a shovel. I have seen some really bad things—rape, robbery, murder, dishonesty, disability, and death. Having seen so much bad stuff, when I consider the things some people do and the vigorous condemnation that conduct elicits from others, I say to myself, "Hey, that's not so bad."

If two men were to kiss in public, some would be offended. If they were to pray in public, others would be offended.

The phrase, "I am offended," used to be the sort of thing you would see in letters to the editor, where some little old lady would write, "Editor, Dear Sir, I am offended by . . ." We would read these letters and laugh and say to ourselves, "Hey, lady, lighten up!"

Nowadays, being offended has become part of our political debate:"I am offended, so you are not allowed to make that comment!" We have abandoned our society to the *offendeds,* and we no longer laugh at each other. We have become a nation where everyone is either a victim or a suspect and where, above all else, humor is not permitted. Free expression, the open marketplace of ideas, has been replaced by rancor while national unity and accord goes by the boards.

The purpose of *The Jelly Donut Diet Book* is to return us to a greater sense of solidarity. If I am offended by this, and you are offended by that, and he is offended by the other, then a truly great author would realize that it is his duty to restore national unity by writing a book that offends everybody. The book I have written, *The Jelly Donut Diet Book,* is designed to do just that. I expect every reader to be offended by some of what I have written, but I also expect him to be amused as I gore somebody else's ox.

The Jelly Donut Diet Book swims against a strong tide, and I do not expect we will ever again hear any American assert, as Voltaire did, "I disapprove of what you say, but I will defend to the death your right to say it." But if the next time somebody begins to say, "I am offended . . ." and is met with a chorus of "Hey, lighten up," then *The Jelly Donut Diet Book* will have succeeded.

—*Judge Lawrence Grey*

CHAPTER 1

Understanding the Jelly Donut Diet

One of the last courses that I took in college, and one of the best, was taught by a truly excellent teacher, Harrison Butterworth. It was an English class and I don't know how the question came up, but on the first day of class he asked how many people lived in ancient Egypt at the time of the Pharaohs. By merest chance, the night before I had just started reading *The Culture of Ancient Egypt* by Herbert Read, so I knew the population was estimated at between twelve and twenty million.

I raised my hand and gave Professor Butterworth that answer. He immediately asked, "What is your source for that?" and I gave it. He was deflated, the poor man. As both a scholar and a teacher of long experience, he had a stan-

dard spiel ready for the first day of all his classes about the need to know whereof you speak. He wanted his students to pick up the habit of scholarship, of research, of having sources for the answers they gave. He would tell his students on the first day of class not to come in with guesses or hunches or beliefs, but to have done the work so that you could speak with authority.

It was a very effective pedagogical technique. On the first day of class, he would select some student to be the bad example, and the students realized that if they did not want to be treated like the poor goat who answered on the first day, they had better be prepared for Prof. Butterworth's class. On the first day of our class together I screwed things up by actually having a source for my answer, so he was forced to proceed with the spiel using my reply as a good example. As everyone knows, good examples are not of much use in teaching because we learn most of what we know from bad examples. His whole discourse lacked fire. Exhorting students to emulate the good example is nowhere near as much fun as threatening the same kind of retribution that fell on the bad example.

Prof. Butterworth was an excellent teacher and not the sort of person one would expect to hold a grudge, but he did. He brooded and plotted throughout the whole semester, and finally on the second to last day of class he got me. We students had learned our lesson well and throughout the entire semester we always had sources of authority for our positions, answers, and arguments. Perhaps because it was not only the end of the term, but also because I was ending my college career, I got sloppy and made some comment without having a source. Butterworth pounced! He had been waiting all semester for this.

"What is your source for that, Mr. Grey?"

I realized he had me, and I thought desperately for something to support my answer. In a flash it came to me. It was brilliant, an epiphany, and I responded.

"In about ten days the president and board of trustees of Ohio University will confer upon me the degree of bachelor of arts with all the rights and privileges appurtenant thereto. One of those rights is that I may now think of myself as a source. I am source for that answer."

The laugh that rose from Butterworth's belly was strangled in his throat. The laugh was instinctive, but his quick mind interjected the thought that what I said was indeed true. He choked, and sadly, wistfully looked me in the eye, and said, "You give new life to the phrase, 'Consider the source.'" That's what I learned in college—I am a source.

I have gone on to earn other degrees, with other rights and appurtenances, and have picked up a feck or two along the way so that I am no longer the feckless youth I was when I first became a source. I am now a powerful white male so I can say to the reader, "I am the source for all the information in this book."

I am not, of course, a reliable source. A reliable source is one whose identity is described by status, *e.g.*, "a reliable White House source," or "a high management executive." Reliable sources are described by status because if you actually knew their identities, you would know exactly their motive for making the information available and how unreliable it is.

Nor am I a confidential source. A confidential source is a fantasy made up by reporters. Reporters think up confidential sources while out playing golf or hanging around in a bar, and then go back to the office and write stories as if there really were such people. Instead of actually gathering news, they know they can create these fictions and never be called on it. If they are questioned about the reliability of what they have written, they spout pious pomposities about protecting sources and the public's right to know, ignoring the fact that what the public most wants to know is the identity of this anonymous slanderer.

I am a source, but it is still incumbent on you to harken to Prof. Butterworth's admonition to consider the source. Frankly, and in spite of what the president and board of trustees of Ohio University might have led you to believe, I am not much of a source. Consider the previous example. I not real sure that the professor was named Butterworth. It might have been Butterfield, but I have seen so many syrup commercials I am confused. I can assure you, though, that it was Harrison because someone once called him Harry, and it burned into my memory because whatever else is true in this world, Harrison Buttersomething was never a Harry.

As I remember this whole classroom incident, *The Culture of Ancient Egypt* was written by Herbert Read. But it seems to me that Herbert Read wrote about the philosophy of art, and I wonder if he was the guy who actually wrote the book. I am fairly certain that Herbert Read would have wanted to write about the culture of ancient Egypt, and if he did he probably would have told us how many people lived there, and that number would probably have been eight to twelve million or twelve to twenty million.

Some readers might think this to be an appalling lack of integrity, and a distressing disregard for accuracy, but keep in mind that I am the beneficiary of a classical education. *Classica educare beatus sum.* I can say things in Latin, but I am not all that sure that what I say, including the Latin, is all that correct. Also keep in mind that under current standards, I am a victim of a classical education. *Classical educare pernicio sum.* I know all the dead white male stuff—history, integrity, grammar, and competence—but have willingly and gratefully adopted the current standards for scholarship, art, writing, and commentary.

Poets today can get by with stringing words together without regard to rhyme or meter such that it seems the only challenge for the modern poet is orthography and typesetting. Short stories are nothing more than minimalist drivel. Scholars no longer think; they use footnotes. Why then, should I be held to any standard in my writing such as truth, accuracy, or integrity? This book should be judged by today's norm.

The real test of this book is: will it sell? This is the real test of anything under contemporary mores. I must admit that I feel that certain sense of smug satisfaction sitting here knocking this thing out on the computer knowing full well that somewhere down the road you, dear reader, will have shelled out good money for this book. I am pleased because I always consider it a good day when I can use the future perfect tense in a sentence. I also find that not being bound by the traditional standards of accuracy is enormously liberating and empowering for a writer who is not good enough to write fiction and can only write non-fiction.

While much of what I say may not be all that accurate, it is mostly all true as near as I can remember or conjecture. Most of what I say here are facts, and most of those facts have come from reading newspapers. I have not made anything up. I am not deliberately lying to you. Still, old habits die hard, and I do feel I ought to give the reader some basis upon which he can feel he has profited and learned from this book, which is written by a person who knows whereof he speaks.

The reader can rely on this book because it was written by a powerful white male. I am one of them. In the good old days when we powerful white males ran everything, everybody was happy. When a powerful white male spoke, it was assumed he spoke with authority. Times have changed. Being a powerful white male is nowhere near as much fun as it used to be, but we are still the linchpin of modern social commentary. In this age of victimization, everybody's claim about which direction our society should be heading is based on how much they were victimized by powerful white males. We used to be the pole star on which society took its heading, but we are still the point of reference. We are still the pivot upon which the earth is to be moved. Just as Archimedes said, no matter how long your bar of grievances may be, unless it rests on the fulcrum of powerful white male oppression, your lever will not work.

For those of you who find it difficult to rely on anything I say, I will give you a quote from H. L. Menchken to be your guide: "The Puritans of the Massachusetts Bay colony banned bear baiting not because of the harm it did to the bear, but because of the pleasure it gave to the spectators."

If there is anything in this book you cannot understand, or anything that appears to be false, inaccurate, mindless, outrageous, or offensive, just say to yourself, mantra-like, "It's not harm to the bear, but pleasure to the spectator."

Although liberalism is condemned by the conservative tide that is sweeping this country, and although liberalism is belittled by the leftist fascists as the ideology of the dead white males, the liberalism of these dead white males is still the basis for all Western civilization. It is the duty of powerful white males of today, much as it was the duty of dead powerful white males, to do for the lessers of society those things that they cannot do themselves. One of those things is to be able to see the world as a liberal powerful white male sees it.

Since this kind of thinking is absolutely necessary to establish the rightness of one's cause, *cassus justus et pius*, this book shall be your source, your introduction to, and your compendium of powerful white male knowledge. We begin with the Jelly Donut Diet to clear your mind of the obfuscations of modern neologisms where liberalism means cracking down on free expression and conservatism means deficit spending. Once you have mastered the Jelly Donut Diet, you can sit back, have a jelly donut and a cigarette, and all the other things discussed in this book such as nutrition, risk, health, race, gun control, or feminism will become apparent to you.

The topics discussed in the Jelly Donut Diet are random and perhaps may appear to the reader as even a bit disjointed. I initially thought I would assist the reader by arranging these topics in this book into an organized fashion, grouping like topics together, such as history, culture, science, etc., but then I had a jelly donut and decided to hell with it. That's how the Jelly Donut Diet works.

CHAPTER 2

The Jelly Donut Diet

66 **I**f you eat a couple of jelly donuts every day, you will feel better."

This is the basic premise of this book. It is a premise so obvious and so irrefutable that it falls into the class of things that Thomas Jefferson described as self-evident truths. A jelly donut tastes good and you enjoy eating one, so why don't you eat a jelly donut every day? Because the nutrition harpies will swoop down to pluck your eyes out? No, it's worse than that. Nutritionists are not mere harpies, they are banshees who come to steal your very soul. The soul is nourished by contentment and the contentment that comes from having eaten a good meal is anathema to nutritionists. What you enjoy is not good for you, they say.

"These are empty calories."

"It is not nutritious; it is not eating right."

Nutrition

Perhaps we ought to inject a little bit of perspective on nutrition into this discussion of what is eating right.

In the thirteenth century, an army of Crusaders attacked and captured a fort set on an island between two forks of the Nile River in the Nile delta. A counterattack by the Egyptians cut the fort off, and a relief fleet from Acre was destroyed. The Egyptian siege lasted for months, and it was only after scurvy broke out that the Crusaders were forced to surrender. The Crusaders were imprisoned pending, as was the custom of the times, the payment of ransoms. After a short while as prisoners, the Crusaders recovered from the scurvy.

Scurvy is a nutritional disease, primarily a lack of vitamin C. What kind of diet does one need to avoid scurvy? Apparently if one eats a diet similar to that given to thirteenth century Egyptian prisoners, it will suffice.

You get all this advice about proper nutrition as if that were a problem in our society. There is a rare nutritionally related disorder (if I can get a publisher to give me a contract to print this book I may take the time to look up the name) that causes internal bleeding in peripheral blood vessels, particularly in children. The bleeding often occurs in the back of the knee and looks like large bruises. I am acquainted with the disease because I was judge on a couple of medical malpractice lawsuits based on misdiagnosis of this condition.

Kids bruise easily, and in the intolerant and often hysterical society we live, more than one couple has looked at their banged-up child and wondered if the Children Services people would be after them for child abuse. Medical people who are used to bruises on kids know that bruises on the front of the child are often the result of a child running into something. Bruises on the back, however, are almost always the result of something or someone hitting the child.

Thus, when concerned parents take a child with large black-and-blue marks on the back of the knee to the hospital and the staff sees the bruises, the parents are shocked to find that their child is taken away and they are being charged with child abuse. A few months later, the hospital and the doctor are in turn shocked to find themselves the defendants in a malpractice suit for failure to properly diagnose this obscure nutritional disease. It is sort of unfair to hold a doctor liable for failure to properly diagnose a condition that he might see only once in lifetime, but that's the way it is in a society living on a diet of blame, recrimination, fresh vegetables, and no jelly donuts.

Nutritional diseases—that is, real pathologies causing real problems—are rarely seen in American society. One of the reasons is that there is an enormous variety of foods available, but another more important reason is our appetite. The appetite is a delicate, sensitive mechanism controlling the things we ingest. It tells you what to eat and what not to eat. On occasion, a very rare occasion to be sure, you may have a taste for broccoli. You may be at some kind of social event where they have a platter of raw vegetables called crudities, which means in French, "raw, crude, uncivilized people who serve such things to their guests." You will look at piece of broccoli and feel like taking a bite. Invariably, when the broccoli looks good, it tastes good. Your appetite is telling you that you are low on some vitamin or mineral or whatever it is that the broccoli contains. Your appetite says to you, "Eat some broccoli—you'll like it." And you do, and you do.

When you are hungry for something, when you have a taste for something, it is your appetite telling you that you need what that food contains. When you have no taste for the food, it is because you have no need for it. Nothing, for example, tastes as good as that first beer after hard work on a hot day. This is a fact eminently and universally known, but as is often the case with common knowledge, some guy will do a study to see why, or even if, what is commonly thought to be true is true.

In a study on beer, they found that after a hard workout where a person has worked up a sweat, the body is low on electrolytes because the perspiration has carried off too many of these ionized substances, which carry the neural system's electrical current much as the electrolyte in your car's battery carries current. Although sweat is primarily water and you are thirsty, a cool glass of water never tastes quite as good as that first cold beer. The first beer tastes so good because it contains the electrolytes your body is missing. Within minutes, the electrolytic balance is restored; your body reacts like a car battery when it is topped up.

After the first beer, it has enough. It is full. The compelling desire for a beer and the unique satisfaction the first beer brings wane as the appetite signals you the need for electrolytes is over. The second cold beer is never as good.

There is no maxim or command given more regularly or with more imperiousness than the dictate, "You must control your appetite!" This is absolutely wrong. You must let your appetite control you. It tells what to eat, and when to eat, and if need be, even who to eat.

Cannibalism and vegetarianism are at opposite ends of the omnivorous scale, but both are identical forms of the appetite telling people what to eat. Anthropologists have found that cannibalism generally exists in two forms. One is a ritualistic form usually involved in ceremoniously eating one's enemies.

For example, in the middle 1700s the English traders in Virginia were expanding into the Ohio country and had established a trading post at Pickawilany in north central Ohio. The Shawnee chief at Pickawilany was called Old Britain and his name eloquently describes his political sympathies.

The French in Detroit wanted a monopoly on the fur trade in the Ohio country and led a raiding party consisting of a few French soldiers and a large party of Hurons and Chippewa on Pickawilany. A good many Shawnee and all the English traders were killed. Because he was such a great chief and so well respected, the Hurons and Chippewa cut up Old Britain, boiled him, and ate him. Ritual cannibalism.

The other form of cannibalism is nutritional and generally only exists among peoples who live in areas where for one reason or another there is not enough protein in the diet. A person living in such an area gets messages from his appetite telling him he needs more protein. He develops a taste for it. He hungers for it. Eventually, he gets around to the same realization as that of the tribal chief in the Flanders and Swan song, *The Reluctant Cannibal*, who argues, "If God did not want us to eat people, He would not have made them out of meat." Nutritional cannibalism.

Vegetarianism is the opposite side of the same coin, and vegetarian people come in all forms, but to understand vegetarianism one must ask this basic question. Have you ever met a vegetarian who didn't like vegetables? There are lots of people who do not much care for vegetables and hardly eat them at all—the meat-and-potatoes crowd. Vegetarians on the other hand, like vegetables and eat nothing but vegetables. This is a fine thing. Vegetarians listen to their appetite and eat what they like. Vegetarians rarely suffer from any nutritional disorder because they are eating what their bodies need. They may have a problem when living in a meat eating society where the foods and combinations of foods necessary to create long-chain proteins are not always readily available, but with a little effort, that problem is easily overcome.

Many traditional folk dishes were actually a result of an unknowing response to the appetite. Corn bread has been traditionally served with beans because the corn contains part of a long protein molecule and beans contain the

other part. Corn bread and beans became popular because
they tasted good together; that is, because the appetite told
people this is what you need. What you need to eat is
almost always what you want to eat.

Vegetarians are usually content because they eat what
they like. This is not to say that too many vegetables do not
have side effects. Much as cholesterol clogs the arteries
bringing blood to the heart, too many vegetables seems to
cause a reduced flow of blood to that part of the brain
which regulates excessive growth in self-importance and
moral righteousness. Vegetarians who eat only what they
like, and who assiduously avoid what they don't like, take
the moral high ground and throw thunderbolts of derision
and condemnation on those others who, just like the vegetarians, eat what they like, too. Judgment is passed on
nonvegetarians who do not eat the right things, and right
is defined not in terms of nutrition, or even nutritional disease, but right in the moral sense.

Eating Right

The idea of eating right is a recent construct, and an idea
that can only arise in the minds of people who have plen-
ty to eat. Traditionally, historically, and especially prehistor-
ically, when a person's major concern was eating as
opposed to not eating at all, the phrase "good food" was
almost a tautology. If it was food at all, it was good—good
to have, good to eat. Remember the classic line about how
hungry the guy was who first cracked open the shell of a

raw oyster and ate what he found inside.

Food is more than nutrition. Food is the affirmation of the good life, and a continual supply of food is a reaffirmation that the good life will continue. All of civilization grows out of the contentment that comes from having eaten a good meal. Without the sense of contentment, the human spirit can never soar to aesthetic heights and the human mind can never achieve the deep reflective state of mind we call philosophy.

Anthropologists, with deference toward the sentiments of people who fund their research, use the term hunter-gatherer to refer to our ancestors. It has a nice ring to it and sounds a whole lot better than the more accurate omnivorous scavenger. The concept of eating right had more narrowly defined parameters in the pre-neolithic days.

Consider the case of two prehistoric hunters who go out each day seeking food for the family. The first hunter comes upon a rabbit sitting quietly in grass, quaking as rabbits do. A quick bash to the head, and he has the rabbit. Holding it by the head, he twirls it a few times. The soft tissues of the rabbit's neck tear as the weak rabbit spine separates and the carcass flops to the ground. A quick couple of gashes with a sharp stone and the rabbit is disemboweled and skinned. He has food for the family.

The second hunter has more trouble finding his rabbit. He flushes a few and throws his spear many times, but rabbits are fast and it is only by merest luck that he momentarily grazed one with the spear point. He is on it an instant before the rabbit can recover, spins the head, and dinner goes flying off into the grass.

Here we have the hunter-gatherer question of eating right. The first hunter knows that if a rabbit is sitting still and not running at the first sight of a predator, he might be sick. He knows that there is some risk in eating a sick rabbit for whatever caused the rabbit to be sick may also cause the hunter's family to be sick. He must take the risk of course, because life is full of risk, and the main risk is not eating. But as he eats the rabbit and as he watches his wife and children eat, he worries. "Are we eating right?" His concern about his family will overpower all other thought.

Hunter two, however, will have no such concern. He knows he has a healthy rabbit. Great hunter that he is, he struck down that rabbit in the prime of its life, and it is good food for his family. He sits contentedly with a full belly watching his kids pick at the bones, and moves a log on the fire. He thinks about how good life is. He leans back and relaxes, thinking about what a nice cave they have, and his eyes wander to the large blank wall of the cave. His fingers are greasy with the fat of the rabbit and black with the soot from the log he moved. The aesthetic impulse is on him and he goes to the wall and draws a picture. All art had its origin in the mind of the contented eater.

Perhaps our rabbit hunter is in a more reflective frame of mind and thinks back to a time when he was a boy and how his father taught him to hunt rabbits. His son has no recollection of his grandfather who died before he was born, so the father feels compelled to tell the boy of his lineage. The hunter recognizes that his father was just a decent, ordinary sort of man, and so he exaggerates and embellishes the truth a bit. From that urge to embellish, all fiction and drama had it roots. And if the grandfather was a scoundrel and a wretch, the father will avoid the truth and resort to fabrication, fantasy, and outright lying; thus, we had our first historian.

The son, also content with his full belly, tells his father he wants to go with him on the next hunt, but the father puts him off saying his arm is too short for a good spear throw. "When you are older, and your arm is longer, you will be able to throw the spear farther," says the father. The boy thinks to himself, "When my arm is longer, I will throw better, but I do not want to wait." Out of this passing thought in the mind of well-fed boy who has time to reflect comes the throwing stick—a device attached to the end of a spear that increases both power and accuracy—the first tool to improve human productivity and the genesis of all engineering.

Not much has changed. Some people will eat and enjoy and will find contentment in a good meal. Others will sit down to the table—a table which has never seen sick rabbit, a table set with a variety foods crammed full of vitamins, minerals, and the various trace elements needed to be healthy, a table with inspected food from the far corners of the earth—and worry about the food they are to eat.

Where does this worry come from? The nutrition harpies and the vegetable Puritans hang over the dinner table like the chorus in classical Greek theater chanting,

"Doom, doom, doom awaits the hubris of enjoying food."

We are continually told that we must eat fresh fruits and vegetables every day. Think about that for a minute. When in the evolution of man did we develop the need for fresh vegetables every day? We are the direct descendants of those hunter-gatherer omnivorous scavengers who only ate fruit and vegetables in season.

Fresh fruits and vegetables—what nonsense! Real nutrition is based on fat. And the best source of fat is the jelly donut.

Using the Jelly Donut Diet

Your author hesitates to suggest a diet for the reader because if there is one rule that is true for all people and for all times, it is this: diets don't work. On the other hand, diet books sell well, which is why I have entitled this book *The Jelly Donut Diet Book.*

Every year or two someone comes out with a new diet book that sells like hotcakes. "Selling like hot cakes" epitomizes this book. If there were a simile, "Selling like broccoli," this book would never have been written. Readers of this year's new hot diet book slavishly follow the dictates of the book's recommended diet. Some of them may loose a few pounds and some even lots of pounds, but invariably they gain it back after a while. While this may be distressing for people who buy diet books, it is great for people like me who write diet books and live, fat and happy, off the fat of the land in fat city. It is with some hesitation, therefore, that I write the definitive diet book, the diet book to end all diet books, because unlike all other diets, the Jelly Donut Diet works!

All other diets do not work because they fail to supply the dieter with all that is needed for a healthy and happy life. Consider the presumptuousness of most diets. They tell you what you should eat. What gall! Recommended diets are the ultimate in one-size-fits-all thinking. They are invariably based on a study that examines the habits of a few thousand people and then statistically extrapolates from the data. But the essence of statistics is that the individual does not count. Indeed, if an individual datum deviates too far from the norm, the statistician picks him off like an antelope who strays too far from the herd. Diets based on norms are totally useless.

One could find a norm for what is required for a good wife, but what use is it? As a lawyer and a judge, I have handled 900 or 1,000 divorces but I haven't a clue as to what makes some marriages successful while others fail. Well, maybe I do have a clue. People who get divorced don't like each other. People who stay married do. Therefore, the only true rule in marriage is marry someone you like.

The only true rule for a good diet is: eat what you like. The Jelly Donut Diet works because it supplies that one element necessary to the good life—satisfaction. Eat what you like. Eat what you like every day. Eat a couple of jelly donuts every day, if, of course, you like jelly donuts. If you like something else, eat that. Eat what you like.

All this talk about eating right is valid only to extent that you learn what is right for you. Whatever you eat, you will get calories, vitamins, and minerals. Whether you get any satisfaction out of what you eat is another thing entirely. Ask yourself this: Do I feel a lack of calories, vitamins, or minerals in my daily life? Do I feel a sense of satisfaction in my daily life?

The satisfaction I speak of is not the moral satisfaction of doing good. I went to high school with a couple of guys, Pete and Charlie. Pete went into business and made a fortune. Charlie became a Trappist monk. Charlie has dedicated his life to God, to prayer, poverty, and sacrifice. He has withdrawn from the pleasures of the world. He eats a simple diet of very little meat, whole grains, and vegetables. During Lent Charlie becomes a vegan because the Black Fast, as it is called, eschews all animal products. Pete lives well, travels first class, and eats in the finest restaurants— on a diet of very little meat, whole grains, and vegetables. The only difference in their eating habits is that when Lent is over, Charlie eats better.

American society is not only serving God and mammon, it is serving them the same things to eat.

The Jelly Donut Low-Fat Diet

Remember our hunter-gatherer? He was not often fat, but worked hard at getting there. The capacity to store fat is a human attribute that has served us well in the past. In the pre-neolithic days, it was always feast or famine. A dead mammoth was the first all-you-can-eat restaurant, and you did eat all you could because you didn't know where your next meal was coming from. The body converted some of it into calories for current use, but then continued to digest and turned all those excess calories into fat—but the fat had to be stored somewhere.

On some people, the body stored in rings around the midsection. On others, it applied it to the hips and buttocks. Then a strange thing developed. For the women with rings of fat, pregnancy became even more difficult. Not only did they have the baby hanging out there, the roll of fat was cantilevered even farther out, aggravating the situation. For men whose metabolism added the fat to their hips and butts, they were quite literally dragging ass on the hunt. After a few hundred millennia of this, it turns out that all the fat-waisted women and all the fat-butted men died off, and we have Homo sapiens as they are today—a species composed of men with spare tires around their waists who breed with women who have fat asses.

Men have a way of dealing with this. They have belts. As the fat accumulates, they let out the belt another notch. Eventually though, every man has to face the fact that he has a big spare tire around his middle, which is hanging over the edge of his belt. But he faces the problem rationally. He buys a bigger belt.

Women seem unable to deal with this. They diet, they jog, they exercise. A woman will, like a man, buy a bigger size, but she will never accept the inevitability of it all.

For the woman faced with this inevitability, I can recommend only one thing. Eat a couple of jelly donuts, which are a part of your low-fat diet. You will feel better, and it will clear your mind and allow you to recognize that, as a direct descendant of those fertile females who first walked upright, no matter what you eat it becomes in the nature of things, low-fat.

LOW-FAT DIET

Losing Weight

The Jelly Donut Diet works because it supplies that one element necessary to a good life—satisfaction. Your job may stink, your spouse may not appreciate all you do, your kids may hate you, your mother-in-law may be a pain in the ass, but none of this affects how good a jelly donut tastes. None of this affects how much you need to have some little thing every day that gives you pleasure. Eat a couple of jelly donuts every day. You'll feel better.

But what about losing weight? How does the Jelly Donut Diet work for that? First of all, if you have enough satisfaction in your life, you won't be all that concerned about what you weigh or getting vicarious opinions on how you look. Secondly, if you eat what you want, you're not likely to eat too much. Your appetite will want you to eat what you need, and what you need is just enough and never too much.

But it is not unthinkable that even in your state of self-satisfaction, you may think about shedding a few pounds. If this happens, eat a couple of jelly donuts and the feeling will probably go away. If it doesn't, then you can go into the Jelly Donut Diet slimming regime, which is quite simple. Eat one jelly donut every day, enjoy it, and say to hell with the rest of it.

The Jelly Donut Diet Exercise Plan

Exercise is like brushing your teeth. It is good for you. It is something you should do every day. But it is also a gross, disgusting thing to watch and you should never do it when other people can see you. People who would never impose on the others the sight of themselves brushing their teeth have no qualms about exercising in public.

People who work out in gyms or health clubs are not too bad. While they do engage in their fitness ablutions in front of other people, they confine their activities to enclosed spaces and inflict their sweaty zeal only on others so inclined. I am willing to accept that health is the new piety but I cannot abide those health pharisees intent on demonstrating to the world that they are fitter-than-thou. Joggers and cyclists are the worst offenders. The joggers are the new monks; the cyclists the new Jesuits.

Joggers are intent on running in the streets, even where there are sidewalks or ovals at a nearby playing field. Joggers, in keeping with the monastic tradition of contemplation and shutting out the world, carry Walkmans and put on earphones to withdraw from the ordinary cares of the world such as how do you avoiding hitting these assholes when driving to work. Joggers dress themselves in brightly colored suits so, they say, that they can be seen by motorists. They want to be seen by motorists not so much to avoid being run over (that's easily done by staying the hell off the street), but rather they want to be seen by motorists as practicing the new religion. We jog. We are fitter-than-thou.

Cyclists are the new hard-driving Jesuits, and in keeping with the modernism of the Jesuits have applied mechanical advantage to make themselves an even bigger pain in the ass. The true cyclist has a bike with a dozen gears to make it more efficient. Making a bike more efficient is moronic. A person who lifts weights for exercise does not use mechanical advantage. If you can lift 150 pounds, you could also rig a block and tackle with a 150-pound pull to lift a 600-pound weight. You would get the same workout, but it would be damn silly. When you gear up a bike with gears and derailleurs and the like, you go can go faster, but if you want to go fast on a bike, put an engine on it. If you want exercise, get an old-fashioned bike with balloon tires and a Bendix pedal brake.

So why are cyclists so enamored of high-geared, high-speed bicycles? Again, they are fitter-than-thou. But unlike the monastic joggers who are merely targets, Jesuitical cyclists find that by gearing up they can pontificate to the whole world. Joggers are limited to being a pain only to their neighbors. Riding a bike expands the opportunity, but even that has its limits because eventually you get tired. But if you gear it up to a high-speed, long-distance vexatious machine, you can bother people all over town. Not only that, you can both annoy motorists and endanger pedestrians, thus demonstrating your fitness to a much larger group.

As I said at the beginning, exercise is good for you, and it gives you a sense of well-being, but we should not lose sight of the benefits of exercise, or how to achieve those benefits. The main purpose of exercise is to get the heart pumping a bit faster, to expand the lungs, and to force blood through the muscles. A good exercise workout leaves you slightly out of breath and your muscles feeling vaguely sore.

As with most things relating to good health, too much can be counterproductive. Exercise can be like dope. The more you engage in it, the more it takes to satisfy your craving. If you jog five miles a day, pretty soon you can do so without being out of breath, without any soreness in the muscles. So you have to go to six or seven miles a day to achieve any benefit. And then it goes to nine or ten. Larger and larger doses, just like heroin.

Compare that with the ordinary follower of the Jelly Donut Diet who appreciates the value of the sedentary life. It is quite easy and far less time-consuming for the Jelly Donut Dieter to reach the stage when one begins to pant and the muscles ache. Having avoided the excesses of the jogging shoes, the weight room, and the bicycle, it takes far less effort to get the old heart pumping. And, of course, smoking helps, too.

It is not within the spirit of this book to recommend any exercise plan for all readers, but one should not denigrate the benefits of walking. If you follow the Jelly Donut Diet, walking can be a wonderful exercise. If it is done right, of course. Begin every morning with a walk down to the corner store and buy a jelly donut. You will feel better.

CHAPTER 3

Smoking

It is important that the reader pay attention here because what follows is of great historical importance. This is the last time anyone will publish a few good words about tobacco. I am doing it while it is still legal.

According to several studies by the National Institutes of Health, nicotine not only increases intellectual performance, it also reduces stress and suppresses aggressive behavior. When two small studies found these soothing side effects of nicotine, the NIH was not at all satisfied with the results. They did a third study, a much larger one, and when it came back with the same results, they stopped doing them.

Still they were left with the question of what to do with the studies. They considered the idea of decreeing these studies to be anathema, but being scientists and having Galileo as a minor god in their pantheon, they rejected the idea. Being bureaucrats, however, they had no difficulty in suppressing the studies in the interest of public health. It is said that one must give the devil his due, but in the free and open society we live in it is heresy to say anything good about tobacco. Demon tobacco has replaced demon rum with the prohibitionists amongst us.

If you doubt the validity of these studies, consider this. As our society has become more and more smoke-free, it has become more rude, intolerant, and aggressive. The newspapers are filled with stories of rage. There is air rage, workplace rage, road rage, this rage, and that rage. Rage is all the rage.

Nobody, of course, can talk about the most obvious cause of this rage epidemic in our society. I would suggest the following. If secondhand smoke is powerful enough to cause cancer, a dubious mathematical projection, it must also cause lesser effects like reducing tension and stress. We have rage because nonsmokers are not getting their soothing dose of nicotine from secondhand smoke.

We have banned smoking in many places where smokers and nonsmokers used to comingle, like offices and airports, but we have not eliminated the ennui and stress common to these places. And now, there being no secondhand nicotine to soothe the savage breast, we have seen the growth of rage in both places.

Post hoc ergo propter hoc. "After this, therefore because of this," is a common fallacy meaning that just because one thing follows another, it does not mean the first caused the second. Perhaps I am wrong about the soothing effects of secondhand nicotine on nonsmokers, but nobody has as yet come up with another potential cause for the rise of rage in our society. That society is jammed to the gills with scientists and intellectuals who ought to be able to spot the cause of rage, but again the deprivation of the beneficial of effects of nicotine are apparent. Nicotine improves intellectual performance. It helps people think and be creative. Would anyone seriously challenge the decline of intellectual performance in our smoke-free universities?

A lot of people can remember when everybody smoked and life seemed better then. When political deals were cut in smoke-filled rooms, people had respect for the government and what it did. Today in the anterooms of our legislatures, the air is pure, but the political deals are polluted. When a cigarette or a cigar was the finishing touch to a good meal, people enjoyed dining. Dining has been replaced by eating right, so enjoyment of either a good meal or a cigarette afterwards is out. Offering someone a light, or even a cigarette, was a small kindness among strangers. Nowadays, strangers are to be feared and definitely not to be approached—not a bad rule of thumb in a world where everybody is tense and aggressive. In our smoke-free world you are less likely to die of lung cancer to some extent because some uptight lunatic will kill you first.

Over the last few years, on the editorial page of the *New York Times*, there has been a series of ads directed at young people about the dangers of smoking. I wonder who wrote those ads and if they have ever talked to a teenage kid. The ad read something like this: "3,000 teenagers will start smoking today. 1,000 of them will suffer serious health effects from it, and another 1,000 will die from it." First of all, talking to kids about death is useless; they simply cannot comprehend it. Second, talking to kids about what might happen when they are sixty is futile because although they can comprehend, vaguely, being old, being old means thirty. And finally, what this ad implies is that if you start smoking now, the odds are one in three that smoking will do you no harm at all.

This actually is the truth. About a third of the smokers die from smoke-related causes, and another third suffer adverse consequences, but the remaining third of the smokers enjoy cigarettes all their lives and suffer no adverse consequences. When you're young and immortal, this ad makes smoking look like a good thing. That the anti-smokers pay for such an ad only enforces my nicotine-deficit thinking argument.

The U.S. Army has gotten in on the health hysteria and is doing all that it can to keep its soldiers, particularly the recruits, from smoking. Banning smoking, or doing every-thing short of banning smoking, is justified by the claim that it reduces the Army's overall health-care costs. This seems a dubious claim since almost all harmful effects from smoking are long-term, but let us suppose it is true. Having soldiers think about their long-term health prospects is a bad idea.

Imagine some kid sitting in a tank on the border of North Korea. He has to be bored out of his mind, sitting there doing nothing, engaged in the same conflict that his grandfather fought. He is likely to think about girls, sports, going home, and the sort. The worst possible thing he can be thinking about is his long-term health prospects. If he looks across the DMZ, he will see an enormous army arrayed against him. The 38,000 American troops in Korea do not compare to the 1,500,000-man North Korean army, and even if you count the 300,000 South Koreans, they are still outnumbered four to one. If war breaks out, his long-term health prospects are poor at best. Even the slowest tank driver is going to realize that his long-term health prospects are best when he turns that tank around and gets the hell out of there.

Do you want our country defended by a bunch of guys who are primarily concerned about their health? Not me. I want them thinking about fighting the good fight and dying a glorious death. When the sergeant yells "Go!" or charge or whatever it is sergeants yell, I want the soldiers out of the trenches and moving forward without pondering about just how risky it is to be doing this. If you condition a soldier to think that secondhand smoke is unacceptably dangerous, what is he to think of secondhand bullets?

In World War II, the Army passed out cigarettes to its soldiers and they, huffing and puffing, went forward and won. The Greatest Generation all smoked, and wonder of wonders, there are still some of them alive fifty years later.

Addiction

But cigarettes are an addiction, and we must stamp out addiction. One of the cardinal truths of the anti-smoking campaign is that tobacco is the most addictive of all the drugs people use. Heroin addicts and pill poppers can get treatment and get the monkey off their backs. Alcoholics Anonymous has done marvelous work. Few, if any, programs have much success with smokers, however. It is, they say, because tobacco is the "most addictive drug."

The "they" who say this haven't a clue about addiction or why people become unaddicted. AA prides itself on being an entirely volunteer organization, but nobody goes to an AA meeting voluntarily. They are there because they have screwed up bad, because they have made a shambles of their lives, and because the harm drinking is doing to them and their families is a present condition. Nobody stops drinking because it might cost him his job in a few years. No one at an AA meeting talks about how his wife might leave him if he keeps coming home drunk and beating her up. People go to AA meetings because they are in immediate danger of, or already have, lost the job or the spouse. It is the current damage that causes people to foreswear an addiction.

But, the addictionists argue, some smokers continue to smoke even after they have been diagnosed with lung cancer. True enough, but smoking is a way of dealing with stress, and lung cancer is stressful. From a practical standpoint, it was past smoking that caused the cancer and current smoking doesn't do that much harm.

Addiction is, by definition, a compulsive behavior, and I suppose we would be better off if we could suppress compulsive behavior, but if we are to stamp out addiction and compulsive behavior, let's begin with the addictive habit of trying to save others from their wicked and evil ways. The people who started the Spanish Inquisition were doing good, they were saving the heretics from the terrible prospect of losing their immortal souls. The mere fact that these heretics, mostly Jews, were tortured and burned here on earth doesn't amount to much when eternity is your highest value. The American Indians suffered and lost a lot of land as a result of the expansionist policy of the United States. They suffered most, however, when the policy shifted from hostility to doing good for the Indians, to save them from their evil habits, and to civilize them.

Peoples have different values. People have different values. The Spaniards could have left the Jews to their temples and practices without endangering their own immortal souls. The Army could have left the Indians to their traditions without imperiling Western Civilization. In a similar vein, the nonsmokers could leave alone those for whom good health is not the highest value. There are those who relish the idea of living a long life. For those of you who look forward to living long enough to end up lying senile and incontinent in a nursing home, perhaps you can cut a bit of slack to others not so inclined.

I recognize that some people don't like smoke, much as others don't like loud radios and such. The ban on smoking in some places is acceptable, but the ban on smoking in places where nonsmokers don't have to be is intolerant.

Fag Bars

Some of us can remember when everybody smoked and homosexuals were suppressed, and we have come full circle to where smokers are the pariahs and homosexuals are just people. As a teenager, I had the opportunity to become a homosexual or a smoker. Unfortunately, I chose smoking. I can add this to the long list of things entitled, "If I only knew then what I know now."

We are bombarded with exhortations about the evils of smoking and at the same time are told that being homosexual is just another form of human behavior.

The odd thing about this is that the very arguments used against homosexuals have a lot of deja vu about them. I can remember a priest, a decent, kindly man who thought homosexual activity was immoral and viewed homosexuals as poor misguided sinners, explaining to me why I should avoid homosexuals. Homosexuals did not reproduce so if there was to be enough homosexuals to go around, they had to recruit new practitioners.

I was about fourteen at the time and this whole homosexual business threw me. I was trying to work out some kind of *modus vivendi* with girls, and it was not going particularly well, so the idea that there might also be sex with men, and that I might be recruited into it, was disconcerting. The idea that homosexuals have to recruit new initiates is now considered a foolish, if not pernicious, idea. We accept the fact that certain people are predisposed to homosexual activity even though most of us can't see the fascination in it. That is just the way they are.

Today, the recruiters of children are the tobacco companies. That is, they used to be the tobacco companies. Today, it is Big Tobacco, because it is much easier to dump on someone after you have demonized them. Big Tobacco must recruit teenagers we are told, told by people who are nowhere near as kindly or tolerant as the priest, because as smokers die off or quit, new smokers have to be recruited. The idea that certain people are predisposed to smoke just as others are to be in love with a person of the same sex is unthinkable. No one ever says about smokers, "Hey cut them some slack. That's just the way they are." Not even the nonsmoking homosexuals.

One of the problems with the anti-smoking campaign is that people who smoke are merely called smokers. There is no pejorative for these people. For almost every other group there is a politically correct name and a pejorative name. Fundamentalist = religious fanatic. Conservative = redneck. Liberal = bleeding heart. But for smokers, we only have "smokers."

Since the homosexuals aren't using the name any more, I suggest we start calling smokers fags. "Fag" as a word has a traditional pejorative connotation, combines the old-fashioned word for cigarette with a British nuance, and though only three letters, has a nice four-letter Anglo-Saxon sound to it.

If we could bring back fag, we might be able to bring back fag bars. In the old days of intolerance, homosexual activity was illegal in almost every state and homosexual bars were suppressed as places, in the wonderful language of the law, "of lewd assignation." Occasionally one would walk into a strange bar and see a young boy drinking or two guys sitting very close to each other in a booth. After a bit one would see that it was not a young boy at all, but a woman dressed in men's clothes, and when you saw one guy in the booth put his tongue in the other guy's ear, you would realize that this was not your kind of place.

But still, fag bars were tolerated by both the police and the public as long as they kept a low silhouette. It was a workable blend of puritanism and hypocrisy. The health puritans of today seek to root out all forms of unhealthy behavior. They ban smoking in bars as unhealthy. I am not so much opposed to a ban on smoking in bars as I am enforcing it. Our society should be, as our fathers and grandfathers were, a little more hypocritical about our puritanism.

We should have laws suppressing these places of unhealthy assignation, fag bars. These would be places where smokers could go to engage in their vile practice, but if a nonsmoker wandered in, he would immediately know the dangers of the place. The health department would make an occasional raid, and the cops would assign an undercover cop to go there and talk to people to get information about the fag community.

Homo sapiens have prospered as a species because we have had fire. But with fire comes smoke. A puff of smoke was blown into the face of the hunter-gatherer sitting around a campfire. It filled the caves of cavemen, the man-sions in ancient Rome, and most houses right up until the development of central heating. But even then, there was still smoke in the house because people smoked ciga-rettes. For the first time in history, people are living in smoke-free environments, and asthma in children is on the rise. I wonder what the cause might be?

At the beginning of the chapter I said I would be saying something nice about tobacco, so I cannot end without saying it. People enjoy smoking. It gives them pleasure. It may be a bad bargain because of its deleterious effects, but if you start smoking at fifteen and smoke a pack a day for fifty years, that's 365,000 cigarettes. If you enjoy just five puffs per cigarette, that's 1,825,000 hits of pleasure.

And to paraphrase Mencken, "The Puritans ban smoking not for the harm that it caused lungs, but for the pleasure it gives to the smokers."

CHAPTER 4

Feminism

One day God came to Adam in the Garden of Eden and said to him, "Adam, I know you are lonely, so I have decided to make you a woman."

"You will be pleased with the woman I will make for you. She will be beautiful and sexy. She will be intelligent, gracious, and charming. She will be the perfect helpmate for you and will do whatever she can to make your life pleasant, comfortable, and productive."

"God," said Adam, "that sounds wonderful."

"There is, however, a price," said God. "To make a woman like that it will cost you an arm and a leg." Adam thought for a moment and said, "Gee that seems like an awful lot. What sort of woman can I get for a rib?"

Fetching Coffee

The justices on the United States Supreme Court have a room where they gather to discuss and decide the cases before them. There is a coffeepot in that room, actually a very handsome antique silver coffee urn that dates back to days when people who could afford such lovely accouterments could also afford servants to bring them their coffee. Because of the need for privacy and confidentiality in discussing the cases, no servants were allowed in the conference room, so the tradition was that the new guy, the least senior member of the court, fetched coffee for the other justices.

When Thurgood Marshall became a justice, his colleagues felt embarrassed by having a black man serve them coffee, so they abandoned the tradition and now each justice gets his own coffee.

Justice Marshall's colleagues would not extend to him the courtesy of that tradition because they were unable to treat him simply as just another guy. Instead he was treated primarily as a black man by a bunch of white men who saw some kind of symbolism in having him serving coffee to powerful white males. Left out of their consideration of this tradition was that Marshall would not be low man forever, that as soon as one of these codgers died off, he would move up the seniority totem pole.

In fact, just three years later Harry Blackmun, a white man, was appointed and became the new low man. If there is some symbolism in having a black man bring a white man a cup of coffee, isn't having a white man bring a black man a cup of coffee at least as symbolic?

Having the new guy fetch the coffee was not such a bad idea because there is nothing more likely to turn a lawyer or judge's head as being nominated for the Supreme Court. The mere mention in a newspaper article that your name is on the list of possible nominees inflates one's status enormously. To be the actual nominee, to get through the Senate confirmation process, and to make it to the pinnacle of the legal profession can only swell the ego. When the new justice with the swelled head arrives in the conference room, it has a salutary effect to have one of the other justices say to him, "You're the new guy here. Get me some coffee." It gives the justice a renewed sense of perspective to remind him that prestigious as the totem pole is, he is still low man.

The result of having done away with this traditional reminder for Supreme Court justices is reflected in the opinions that have been handed down in the last thirty years.

We now have a couple of women justices and nobody fetches them coffee either. As a matter of fact we now have women moving up all the totem poles in all areas of American society. Women not merely as doctors, or professors, or executives, but women as chiefs of surgery, or department heads, or CEOs. But even as there are more and more women at or near the top of the totem pole, they do not seem to be enjoying the same level of job satisfaction that we powerful white males have enjoyed in these same positions. They have good reason for feeling shortchanged. Nobody fetches them coffee.

The feminists have ruined it for women. In the good old days one could, if one were powerful enough, ask a secretary to bring you a cup of coffee, and the coffee brought to your desk not only satisfied your need for caffeine but reinforced your superior status. But under early feminism, this came to be a demeaning request and an affront to the secretary's dignity because it reinforced her lowly status. A secretary's status was lowly, and indeed it still is, but in every work situation someone is low man on the totem pole.

When I worked on construction, I was often the guy they sent to get coffee. Aside from being a part-timer (I worked on construction to get through college and law school), I was also relatively weak so that, in the minds of most foremen taking me away from work rather than some strong guy was more efficient. Although being the coffee fetcher reinforced my status as the lowest guy on the job, I was never offended by this, partly because then as now I believe in a hierarchy on the job, but mainly because carrying coffee and donuts is a hell of a lot easier than carrying bricks or shoveling concrete.

Feminists, however, were offended by having to get coffee. It demeans women they said, and so the idea that it is more efficient and reasonable to have the lowest-paid employee get the coffee went by the boards. The secretary's lowly status is no longer reinforced by having to get coffee, but along with this comes the entailment that the department head's status is no longer reinforced by having his, or her, coffee fetched.

When one uses the politically correct phrasing, "the department head's status is no longer reinforced by having *his or her* coffee fetched," the results of the efforts of the feminists are demonstrated. Feminists have created a world where one must always use "his or her" when you mean the third person indefinite "his," even though nobody will ever bring a woman CEO "her" cup of coffee. They are hoist on their own petard of workplace equality.

Let me make a small digression here. Everyone has heard the expression, "Hoist on his own petard," but according to an informal poll I conducted among people who have heard of the phrase and even some who have used it, few seem to know what it means. A petard was an old-fashioned weapon used to attack an enemy battlement and worked kind of like a hand grenade. A petard was a bomb packed with gunpowder and wrapped in shrapnel. It was tied to a long pole with a loose knot and enough rope to reach over the enemy wall. The fuse was lit, and the attacker would run toward the wall and swing the pole against the top of the wall. The centrifugal force carried the bomb forward, and when the pole's movement was abruptly halted by the edge of the wall, the loose knot would break, and the petard would fall into the enemy ranks and explode. Sometimes the knot on the petard was tied too tight and did not break loose, so the poor schmuck ended up running around with a bomb over his head and no way to get rid of it. He was hoist on his own petard.

Or, nowadays, he or she was hoist on his or her own petard. But if one looks at the feminists besieging the walls of power, one sees dangling from the petard not a bomb but a coffee maker.

"HOIST ON HER OWN PETARD"

Low Self-Esteem in Young Women

An apparently recent problem brought to our attention by the feminists is low self-esteem in young women, more accurately described as high school girls. Girls who do well in elementary school and junior high begin to fall behind in high school. They become poorer students, anorexic, bulimic, and suffer all sorts of losses to their self esteem.

The feminists assign several reason for this phenomenon

such as the emphasis in the media on the unobtainably slim body, or the stress created by policies in high schools that discount academic achievement by girls. They cite studies that show that boys get called on by the teacher more than girls, for example. Or that girls who do well in math in grade school do much less well with high school math.

As is usual with the problems the feminists bring to our attention, this one is caused by the feminists themselves, and as usual, the obvious solution to the problem is regarded as sexist. Take this calling-on-boys-more argument. You would think that anybody who advanced that argument had never been to high school. The average student, when it appears the teacher is about to ask a question, sits in class looking intensely interested while silently chanting the mantra, "Don'tcallonmedon'tcallonmedon'tcallonme."

The teacher, of course, is scanning the faces of the students to see which one looks most interested. Like a poker player assessing a bluff, the teacher recognizes that the student who appears most interested is probably the one least prepared. Girls, having more likely done their homework and generally being better prepared, are called on less. So what the feminists perceive as a great conspiracy is nothing more than the fact that there are few perqs available to a high school teacher, and one is to dump on some kid who doesn't know the answer. Thus, the teacher usually picks from the pool of bluffers; *i.e.*, mostly boys.

Or take math. The feminists want girls to take more math classes. Can you think of anything more likely to lower your self-esteem than math class? You sit there while the math teacher gives you all this stuff that makes little or no sense, like prime numbers. Prime numbers, numbers that are divisible only by one and themselves, seem to be sort of useless or at least unworkable and ordinary students, both boys and girls, fail to see the wonders of these anomalies. Math class lowers everyone's self-esteem. That's what it is designed to do.

So why do we have this problem with low self-esteem in high school girls today? The main reason is the lack of dirty old men. More exactly, we have become a society that is not all that intolerant of dirty old men and are suffering the effects of that intolerance.

In the good old days, dirty old men were allowed to ogle and drool over high school girls. Many a man has gone to some high school function and wondered at the girls. "It wasn't like this when I was in school," they think. In fact it was, but as the callow youths they were, they didn't realize it. High school boys haven't a clue about the girls around them, and when we limit high school girls' contacts to them, invariably almost all the girls suffer from low self-esteem.

In the good old days, dirty old men (which, by the way, is in the mind of a high school girl anyone over thirty) would occasionally make what were called improper advances. Every girl I knew in high school, except one, told me that they were routinely propositioned when the husband gave them a ride home from babysitting. The one exception told me that whenever the husband offered to drive her home the wife said, "Oh, no you don't."

It was assumed, then, that a guy with a few drinks in him sitting next to a young girl would come on to her. Now, it is a felony and you can go to jail just for asking, although then as now, the likelihood of getting a positive response is a remote as ever.

So am I advocating open season on young women? Not at all. I am a traditional moralist and a firm believer in the moral principle expressed in the law as statutory rape and in the vernacular as jail bait. All I am saying is that if we leave self-esteem in young women to their contemporaries, male or female, or, God forbid, to mathematicians, it will be invariably lower. But if we leave it to leering, dirty old men, it won't be a problem.

Men's Work and Women's Work

To the feminists nothing is more outrageous than the idea that there is, or ought to be, men's work and women's work. The idea that men should do certain kinds of work and should not do other kinds of work is cited as a typical example of the conspiracy to keep women in their place in a male-dominated society. The fact that it has always been this way, even in matriarchal societies, cuts no ice with them. Having men's work and having women's work is society's way of getting dirty jobs done.

Some of the most wretched jobs are also considered the most macho. Cowboys, truck drivers, and coal miners all carry an air of virility about them, but if you give a moment's thought to the actual work they do, and the conditions in which they do it, these occupations are a dreadful way to make a living.

Cowboys ride the range under an open sky and all that, but the reality of the job is that spending hours in the saddle in all kinds of weather is both hard work and dull. There are few animals as dumb as the horse, and one of them is the cow. If you spend your time on a horse among cows, sooner or later you are going be to thrown, kicked, butted, trampled, bitten, or gored. On a bad day, a cowboy might be subjected to all of these occupational hazards. On a good day when nothing of this sort happens, the cowboy can sit back and relax and enjoy the heat, the dust, the burning sun of summer, the cold wind, the freezing drizzle, and the snow drifts of winter that come from the open sky.

Truck drivers have it a little better. The cab of a semi does provide more protection from the elements than the wide brim of a cowboy's hat, but while the cowboy's work is boring the over-the-road trucker's work is absolutely mind-numbing. The constant drone of the engine, the mesmerizing effect of mile after mile of the same dreary, almost identical Interstate lanes, and the constant shifting of gears to adjust for every little variation in grade are bad enough, but on top of that the long-haul truck driver is almost never at home. And all the while they are away from home, they must spend their time among critters even dumber and more ornery than cows or horses—the loonies in cars.

Truck stops have found that they can get drivers to stop and buy gas if they have clean showers for the drivers and a place to rest. These areas are restricted to drivers, but I have examined a few and found them to be basic, but clean, facilities not unlike a new jail in a small town, except for the bars. What kind of job is it where the opportunity to get cleaned up and lie down on a cot for a few hours is regarded as an enormous improvement in the quality of the work environment?

Mining is worse. Although thousands of feet of earth and rock may protect the coal miner from the elements of the open air, it also means that there is no open air. There is only that air which can be pumped down from the surface to displace the lethal, explosive coal gas. The mine is in a constant state of change as the miners go deeper and deeper into the seam, and the most perilous change is that of collapse since all mines collapse sooner or later. If sooner, there are tragic consequences for the miners, but even if later, the mine is a deadly place. Coal mines often leave large pillars of coal unmined so that these pillars can hold up the roof while the remainder of the coal is extracted. The weight of the overburden puts enormous pressure on these pillars, pressure so great that sometimes the face of the pillar explodes and shoots coal into the mine with the force of a cannon. The deepest, darkest, most fetid dungeon of the most notorious castle in the Middle Ages was not as deep, not as dark, not as fetid as the typical coal mine.

The miserable and dangerous working conditions of the cowboy, trucker, and coal miner are not reflected in the pay scale for these occupations, but these men do provide society with valuable and necessary products. So how does society get men to do things that are necessary if we are to have food, transportation, and electricity?

To get men to do anything is not all that easy except when it comes to sex. Somewhere in our distant past, some brilliant genius, undoubtedly a woman, hit upon an idea that has done more for human productivity than any other invention like agriculture or electricity. The idea is so simple: if society can link male sexual identity to dirty, boring, low-paying jobs, the men will be lined up to do them.

Western civilization has been successful and prosperous because we have not only linked sexual identity to work, we have been able to achieve an inverse ratio where the crummier the job, the greater the macho status that goes with it. Cowboy or miner, it is a thing that a man does, and as John Wayne has told us, "A man's gotta do what a man's gotta do."

Women, too, have their share of the occupational nasties. Being a nurse is a terrible job. You must tend to needs of people who are sick, who cough up vile globs of slime, who ooze soporose fluids and excrements, and who hurt bad. Sometimes they die. A friend of my wife, an emergency room nurse, had a baby die as she held it in her arms and in spite of how deeply this affected her, the next day she was back on the job because her sense of being a woman is inextricably tied to being the loving, caring, technically proficient nurse that she is.

Washing dirty clothes is one of those unappealing tasks whose dreariness is compounded by its repetitive nature of week after week. Still, clean clothing significantly contributes to society's sanitation needs and as such is too important not to be assigned to some group whose job it is to see that it gets done. In our society, it has been assigned to women and welded to their femininity.

If a woman were to get up on a Sunday morning and, as Johnny Cash says in his song "Sunday Morning Coming Down," "put on her cleanest dirty shirt," she would be called slovenly and slovenly women are not accepted—not by other women and not even by men. A slovenly man, a bachelor who lives alone perhaps, will be described with kinder adjectives such as rumpled or tousled. A woman, even a woman with a husband and six kids to care for, will not be seen in other than clean clothes unless she is frowzy, dowdy, or unkempt, and under the double standard, she will be held responsible for the cleanliness of her husband's and her children's clothes. No benefit inures to a woman for having herself and her family dressed in clean clothes, but by tying femininity to society's need for clean clothes, and by holding women to this double standard, our societal goal is achieved.

Take the job of cleaning fish, a nasty task if ever there was one. I read a scholarly article about cleaning fish in several different societies that indicated that in every society studied, cleaning fish was either exclusively men's work or exclusively women's work. In no society did both men and women clean fish equally. Does this mean that there never was a society where men and women stood on the ground of fish cleaning equality? Perhaps not. There may have been such a society, but we have no historical or anthropological record of one. If there was such a society, it has vanished from the face of the earth leaving no trace of its existence. From this we can reasonably infer that not only is assigning work based on sex necessary, a society which fails to do so is doomed to extinction.

Even a reasonable feminist, and we will ignore the oxymoronic implications of that phrase, might concede that tying sex to work was not such a bad idea, but she would then ask, if that be true, why is it we got all the nasty jobs, like nurse, or cook, or laundress? Why do we never get any of the statusy, good-paying jobs? First let's look at pay, then at status.

Equal Pay for Equal Work

Nothing drives women so wild as the idea that men are paid more than women for the same work. This is the absolute injustice for them, but as is typical with the arguments feminists advance in favor of their cause, it would appear that they have only the most rudimentary grasp of any subject they wish to discuss.

Work and pay are economic issues, and most feminists act as if they have never read a book on economics. The value of anything is based on its scarcity and the cost is based on the amount of money it will take a person to part with it. If you want to induce a man to part with his labor you have to come up with enough money to induce him to do so.

Men are lazier than women. Any woman will tell you that

men are a bunch of slobs who will not pick up after themselves and sit around the house doing nothing when there
are all sorts of things that need to be done. If what women
say is true, then it will take a greater sum of money to get
men to part with their labor. This is not discriminatory, it is
the immutable law of supply and demand as given to us by
that dead white male, Adam Smith. Men are paid more
because their labor is scarcer.

Women will part with their labor for fewer dollars.
Although they have been assigned more than enough sex-
related duties like cooking, cleaning, and taking care of the
kids, they seem intent on looking for even more work to
do. They want careers. They want challenging, satisfying
work. If the boss knows you want to work to obtain something other than money, he is likely to pay you less. Women
are paid less because their labor is more abundant.

The Glass Ceiling

The feminists also complain that in spite of their efforts to
climb the corporate ladder, and in spite of being just as
good as men, there is a glass ceiling, that invisible but
impenetrable barrier that prevents them from getting to
the top. There may be few token VPs or even a woman sitting on the board of directors, but there are no women
CEOs. This may be true, but there is a reason for that.
Women are physically unfit for such work.

As noted previously, there is no physical reason why
women cannot do men's work. We do have women driv-

ing trucks, digging coal, and rounding up cattle. Although they get no sexual reinforcement out of it, they are physically able to do the work, and one might think that there are no such physical barriers to their doing CEO work. Unfortunately, there is.

There are two kinds of people: those who grow hair on their face, and those who don't.

The Y chromosome carries with it not only the genes that make one male, but the genes that make one engage in peculiar male behavior. While female behavior is generally within well-defined limits, male behavior runs the gamut of peculiarities. Some of these peculiarities are so common that we hardly give them a thought, but when was the last time you saw a woman at a football game paint her big, fat belly with the logo for the Philadelphia Eagles and flash the TV camera with it. Only men are crossdressers. Women will wear men's clothing, but only men get off on it. For men, aberrant behavior is the norm, and at the far reaches of the bell curve for that norm, there is some really aberrant behavior.

Simply put, only men are serial killers. There has been on occasion a woman who commits multiple murders, but these are almost always done for profit like the woman who poisoned four husbands. Compare this to someone like Ted Bundy or John Wayne Gacey, whose serial murders were committed for some incomprehensible reason. The Y chromosome seems to carry with it the tendency to be a serial killer.

How would one describe a serial killer? Let's get out the

thesaurus. Serial killers are secretive, ruthless, aggressive, sly, unfeeling, perverse, and vicious. How does one beat out all the other guys and get to be the CEO? By being secretive, ruthless, aggressive, sly, unfeeling, perverse, and vicious. While all men have the Y chromosome and the potential to become either serial killers or CEOs, most limit their aberrant propensities to football, occasionally wearing their wife's panties, or middle management.

The serial killer/CEO is an odd type of personality with a convoluted and inscrutable world view. None of us really understands why they kill. By the same token, none of us understands how a CEO of a company that has lost 1.2 billion dollars in the last year and whose stock has lost two-thirds of it value can collect a 27-million-dollar performance bonus. Ask yourself this. Where could you find a woman who would do such a thing?

The glass ceiling is there because women do not, literally and figuratively, have the balls for this kind of behavior.

Women's Bodies

In an earlier chapter I explained about low fat as the natural condition of man, but women are overly concerned about body fat. Men and women have entirely different concepts of their bodies, and generally speaking a man is much more likely to be satisfied with his body than a woman is. A woman's concept of her body is much more complex and invariably she is unhappy with it. I shall try to explain the human female body and thus make women happier—a task long incumbent on us powerful white males.

We are, as orthopedists always tell their aching patients, direct descendants of those humanoids who moved on all fours until good old Homo erectus decided to get up and walk around. Unfortunately our bodies have not evolved from the all-fours mode and that stack of bones we call the spine is often knocked out of kilter with painful results. For patients who complain about radiating pain in the muscles and sensitivity or ghost pains in peripheral areas, the ortho- pedist will explain the duality of the nerve system arising out of sharing a common ancestor with the fish.

From a structural standpoint, there is not a lot of differ- ence between men's bodies and women's bodies. Basically both are a squarish arrangement of bones designed to pro- vide support at four points. The hominids who skittered about on all fours rarely had backaches because both the hands and the feet supported the spine.

Standing up on the hindquarters gives you a lot better view of what there is around to eat, and what there is that might eat you, so those who could stand were better able to survive and reproduce. But all this standing about turns the four-square skeletal system into a stack of bones, an inherently unstable structure which, like all stacks, wants to fall over.

Standing, like everything else in life, is subject to the double standard, which means it is good for men and bad for women. Standing gives a man, well, standing. He can see better, run better, fight better, and eat better. Standing does not add much to a woman's ability to do womanly things and is a particular drawback in doing that ultimate womanly thing, being pregnant.

Hominid woman carried their babies in their stomachs. Walking on all fours provided adequate support for the expanding uterus because the foetus was suspended in the center of the four-square skeletal support system. Once women began to stand up, the babies were no longer well supported, but sort of hung out off the front, a biological cantilever. A cantilever is a structural concept used to describe an element that is supported only at one end. It was by studying canti levers that Galileo came up with the idea of pre-calculus. Pre-calculus is still taught today and teaches students to understand why they are going to flunk calculus next semester. Calculus itself is the invention of Isaac Newton, who wrote the *Principa Mathematica* as the underpinning for his Law of Inertia, which describes the effects of teaching mathematics to people who really ought to be majoring in one of the social sciences.

None of us are mathematicians, thank God, but we all understand the basic principle of the cantilever; *i.e.*, the further the unsupported cantilevered end extends, the more pressure there is on the supporting end. You can hold twenty pounds next to your chest, but hold it at arm's length and it seems heavier. You can carry fifty pounds on your back and not get too tired, but trying to carry just five pounds at arm's length soon exhausts the muscles. This increasing pressure on the arm muscles is just the sort of thing you used to plot on graph paper where one line remains fairly constant, while the other curves dramatically.

The bellies of standing pregnant women are cantilevers and the bigger the baby gets, the more likely they are to fall over. Evolving from an all-fours hominid into a standing Homo sapiens made pregnancy even more difficult because of the sapiens part. "Sapiens" means knowing, cogent, thinking, having a brain. The brain is the most important organ of Homo sapiens, and the one most critical to his survival. Bigger brains mean more memory, more thinking, and a greater ability to process all the data coming in from the environment.

Various species have certain attributes and as a general rule, the more any member of that species partakes of that attribute, the more likely it is to survive. All cheetahs are fast, but the fastest cheetahs have the advantage. If having a brain is crucial to the species survival, the brainiest have the advantage. Everyone knows that big babies are healthier than little babies, but birth weight is determined largely by head size and the size of the head is determined by the size of the brain. The brain grows in utero and the skull grows around it.

As the Homo sapiens women were growing bigger babies with bigger heads containing bigger brains, the evolution of the birth canal failed to keep up. This is why of all the mammalian species only women have painful deliveries. This is not a good thing—not for the woman, not for the species. But nature has a way of compensating with wider hips and with more weight on those hips to act as a cantilevered counter balance.

This is the ultimate truth about fat on a woman's body. Women who swim against this evolutionary tide are doomed to failure. Women who eat jelly donuts are in the vanguard of evolution, and much happier.

Men's Bodies

Men are more satisfied with their bodies in whatever shape they are. This is because the male concept of body is more rudimentary. A man's body is the thing attached to his penis. It gets him around so he can use his penis.

If this discrepancy in bodily satisfaction between men and women seems unfair, one must remember that life is not fair, and in any event it should put an end to all this talk about God being a woman.

CHAPTER 5

Race

Some commentators have suggested that blacks still suffer from the lingering effects of slavery and discrimination. There seems to be some truth in this. For example, young black men in our society are so poorly acculturated that they cannot operate a baseball cap.

It is even sadder to watch black men, particularly young black men, trying to shake hands. They seem to be unable to grasp either the idea or the other guy's hand. I have watched their pathetic attempts as they try to shake hands, each time getting it wrong. They close their hands and bump each other's fist a couple of times, and when that doesn't work, they rub thumbs. One will try to tap his fist on the top of the other, and when that doesn't work, the other guy then tries to tap his fist underneath the other's. Finally it occurs to them that they aren't ever going to be able to shake hands unless they open the fists, so they do that, but even then they still have trouble. One guy will raise his open hand to about chest level while the other lowers his to below the waist, and then the upper guy swings his open palm towards the other. This makes a resounding clap, but of course, with open palms there is still no handshake. So they switch and try it again, sometimes two or three times, but still no handshake. Finally realizing that they aren't ever going to get it right, they clasp each other and say, "Bro!"

One of the relics of our unseemly past that remains to haunt us is ribs. The poor people of every culture have an affinity for ribs and it doesn't matter whether they are black, Polish, or Chinese. The way we make ribs, they will tell you, is delicious and you gotta try them. This culinary pride is common to most cultures because they share the same historical background in cutting up the pig.

In the good old days, whether in China or Poland or Georgia, when it came time to slaughter a pig, the meat was divided in the same way. The hams, the chops, and the tenderloins were taken up to the big house owned by the master, or the magnate, or the *yo chin lo*. The ribs and trotters were left to the peasants or the slaves.

The rich guys then, as the rich guys now, were always concerned about class envy. So lords had to convince the serfs that their share of the pig was okay. A slave owner, instead of giving his slaves something to eat, would give them a few cents worth of spices so they could barbecue the ribs. He might even come down from the big house, sample a rib and lick his fingers and say, "Ummm, good!" to convince his slaves they were actually getting something to eat.

Ribs, this vestige of slavery, continues to this very day. Ribs have absolutely no meat on them. Ribs have no net nutritional value. You have to work like a dog gnawing at scarcely covered bones, and you hardly get enough meat to offset the energy and calories burned. Ribs are a fraud on poor people, and Southern-style barbecue ribs are one of the vestiges of the enslavement of black people.

Another vestigial anomaly is that historically blacks were never treated as immigrants in a nation of immigrants. America is not just a nation of immigrants, it is a capitalist nation of immigrants. Wave after wave of immigrants arrived in America seeking a better life and took whatever job was available. The Germans dug the canals; the Irish and the Chinese built the railroads; the Poles and other Slavs dug coal and iron ore and built the steel mills—each group taking its turn at doing what had to be done.

It was not long, however, before it occurred to some of these immigrants that killing yourself with back-breaking labor was not the way to go. They learned that if you could amass some capital, life would be better, and if you had a lot of capital life would be very good indeed. Unfortunately, there are only two ways to get capital: either you save it or steal it, and when you're making twelve cents an hour saving isn't much of an option.

Even more unfortunately, the rich people—the ones who got to America first and had all the money—kept a close eye on what they owned. Thus, the only large pile of money available was the public treasury, so each immigrant group went after that. One by one, each group took its turn to get its snout into the public trough and each availed themselves of this uniquely American method of climbing the social ladder.

To get at the public treasury you have to be an office holder, so the first step is to build an ethnic voting bloc— a well-oiled political machine, and get your people elected. Once in office, public money becomes the oil that keeps the machine working smoothly, until enough money can be stolen to allow the leaders of the immigrant group to set up businesses, buy nice houses, and send their children to college. Thus, their children have entry into business, banking, insurance, and law, where the opportunities for loot far outnumber anything available to a public official.

The second generation, the immigrants' children, are real Americans, and rich Americans at that. They mingle with third-generation immigrants who go to Harvard and Yale and whose grandparents stole fortunes, which passes for old money in America. This second generation lacks their parents' drive. They are not as hungry and have neither the skill nor the interest in looting the public coffers, so the machine grows old and wears out. But waiting in the wings, or more exactly waiting in the slums, there is a new immigrant group ready to run on a reform ticket and eager for their slice of American pie.

This was one of our finest American traditions and a common tie that bound each succeeding immigrant group to both the group that went before and the one that followed. The metaphor of American history is not the melting pot, but the ladle by which everybody in turn got his share. But now this melting pot is gone, and worse yet, there are those who would replace it with multicultural-ism. They say we should look at each immigrant group sep-arately and celebrate their contributions to our society. But the American Dream is not about contributing, it is about getting!

When the blacks' turn came, the historical path to the American dream was not available to them. Their turn came after World War II following an internal immigration from the rural south to the opportunities in the northern industrial cities. They followed the usual path from slum to political organization to machine to elective office, but there was no money to seed black capitalism. The blacks' chances have been stymied because this fine, old tradition is now frowned on by groups like Common Cause and the League of Women Voters. The do-gooders and the good-government types have stopped the process by which eth-nic groups are integrated into the American mainstream, and the problems we have with race relations is probably all their fault.

But the blacks are resourceful and lacking the historical and traditional entree into American society, they turned to professional sports where they dominate.

Every so often, some poor boob brings down a firestorm of criticism upon himself by suggesting that black athletes are in some way genetically different from whites. For example Jimmy the Greek, the Las Vegas odds-maker, was pilloried for saying that blacks did better in professional sports because, during the era of slavery, they had been bred to develop those qualities that would be most useful in sports. What'shisname, the guy who wrote *The Bell Curve,* said the same things using the mumbo jumbo of statistics and sociology and was likewise roundly condemned by one and all.

It is an article of faith in our society—a society with very little faith—that blacks and whites arc not genetically different. To even hint at such a thing will bring out thousands of commentaries, editorials, and letters to the editor denouncing the very thought as racist, and indeed the ultimate expression of racism. All these writers will insist that any difference between black and whites is a result of environmental and socio-economic factors. But then they all stop there. They all say it is environmental, but nobody ever discusses what environmental factors might have led to the domination of professional sports by black people.

There are about 2,900 to 3,000 professional athletes playing football, baseball, and basketball. Of these, about 1,900 are black—almost two-thirds. This two-thirds comes from a segment that is only about 13 percent of the overall population. All things being equal, one would expect about 350 to 400 black players in professional sports, so to even the most obtuse observer a number five times as great as what would be expected indicates that there are powerful forces in our society that created this result. It is odd that such powerful forces are not readily apparent.

Perhaps if we look into the matter seriously and studiously, we can come up with an answer. Let's begin by getting the genetic thing out of the way right off. The idea that blacks are natural athletes, somehow stronger and faster, is an idea that no reasonable person would subscribe to. The only people who think this way are the racist KKK types of whom there are a few, and the black nerds, of whom there are many.

The black nerds are firmly convinced that all blacks, including themselves, are inherently good athletes. Blacks who are really good at sports get scholarships and play professionally. But what about the black nerd, the black guy who catches a baseball with his face. Some go to college and law school and end up playing in the slow-pitch softball lawyers' league. I played on the Legal Aid baseball team, which was made up entirely of liberals, some white, some black, but all nerds. We played teams from the large law firms whose players, some black and some white, were pretty good. The typical career path for one of these big firm stars goes like this. Baseball scholarship to Duke. A year in the minors. Cut. Go to law school, join a big firm, and sign up for the firm's team in the lawyers' league. A law firm with 100 young associates can pick and choose who gets to play.

Our legal aid office could barely field nine players, and then only because the boss cajoled, and then threatened, us into it. He was a good boss, and a good lawyer who dedicated his professional life to service in legal aid. He was also short and fat and a wretched first baseman. A first baseman has to be able to keep his foot on the bag and stretch out and catch wide throws from the field. When you are short and fat and getting a throw from a geek who throws like a girl, being black does not help much. Still he felt he was a great player. Black medical klutzes are the same. I was occasionally asked to fill in for a doctor on a basketball team. I found that the black nerds who become doctors hog the ball and miss shots in the firm belief that they are natural athletes.

Still there must be some reason why black young men are so over-represented in college and professional sports. Perhaps it is because sports is the only activity in our society where a black man is judged pretty much on his own ability. If you're good, you're good—based on your performance. If you're no good, you're no good—no excuses. There is no affirmative action in the NFL or the NBA. In sports, nobody tries to do good for black people, and wonder of wonders, they do pretty well.

OPERATING INSTRUCTIONS

CHAPTER 6

Health and Wealth

There used to be a saying, "I enjoy good health." Now, nobody enjoys good health. They work at it.

Most people have a nice home filled with gadgets and amenities, and our cars come with sunroofs and stereos. Most families can find a few extra bucks for some kind of luxury every now and then. Life is pretty good, and we want for little, but the reality is that almost all of us live from paycheck to paycheck. If the job is lost and the paycheck stops coming in, or even if only one of the paychecks the family depends on stops coming in, the good life soon grinds to a halt.

Prosperous as we are, few of us are wealthy. We live in a capitalist society, but nobody has any capital. On the other hand, there are people who enjoy the good life without having to work for it. The money keeps rolling in no matter what they do. They don't have to work to get the money they need to be comfortable. They are wealthy, and that is what wealth is—having money without having to work at having it.

Health is the same way. Being healthy is not not being sick. Good health is not being sick without any effort on your part. We are told that if you exercise every day, eat your vegetables, avoid fatty foods, and don't smoke you will be healthy. But what kind of health is this? If you have to work at being healthy, you are not healthy. A type 2 diabetic who must continually monitor his diet, blood sugar, and insulin levels is not healthy. Going in for dialysis twice a week is not being healthy. Good health is doing what you want to do. Good health is avoiding what you don't like.

You would prefer to have money without working for it, yet if you still have to work for your money, you are not wealthy. You would prefer not to be sick, but if you have to work at not being sick, you are not healthy. Good health comes from doing nothing. Anything else is medical treatment or physical therapy.

Our perceptions of what good health is has been distorted by the doctors, but they were pushed into doing it by the lawyers. There is a trend in our society to blame every evil on lawyers. As a lawyer myself, I sometimes find this criticism unfair, but in terms of good health, lawyers have been a disaster.

Doctors used to cure some of their patients, but some courses of treatment had bad results and this was accepted as a natural occurrence. Then lawyers started suing doctors for bad results whether or not there was any real malpractice. As a judge I have seen not seen many cases of true malpractice. This is not to say doctors don't screw up. They do, and often with tragic results. But those cases don't get to court; they get settled. Where there has been a bad result, regardless of whether it is the fault of the doctor or not, there will be a trial and the plaintiff's attorney will bring the poor guy into court in a wheelchair and the jury will feel sorry for him and lay on a large chunk of money.

The lawyers have abandoned the concept of negligence in malpractice cases and replaced it with fault; *i.e.*, if there is a bad result, it's the doctor's fault. Because this was happening too often, the doctors who passed on the ever-increasing cost of malpractice insurance decided that they, too, would adopt the fault standard and pass it on to their patients. Now if something bad happens to you, the medical community will say, "It's not our fault—it's your fault."

Medicine

Modern medicine began with the prevention model. Being unable to cure most of the maladies that racked the human condition, doctors started looking for ways to prevent illnesses. When Thomas Sydenham found that almost everyone suffering from an outbreak of cholera in London got their water from a single well, the science of epidemiology was created. If you look at a group of patients and find a factor common to all, there is a good possibility that that common factor is related to, or even the cause of, their sickness. And once you have the cause, prevention is the next likely step. In the nineteenth century, medicine made enormous progress and life expectancy was vastly expanded by simple devices of aseptic procedures, safe water supply and a good sewer system.

In a similar vein, Edward Jenner observed that people got smallpox only once. He also noted that people who had had cowpox never got smallpox. Intuiting the existence of the human immune system and even how it worked, he figured out that if the smallpox did not kill you, your body developed some form of protection against the disease thereafter. If you had cowpox, you had that same kind of protection, but cowpox was a much less virulent disease, and almost never fatal. Thus, if doctors could induce cowpox in all their patients, none would get smallpox. The Latin name for cowpox is *vaccinia*, from which came vaccinations from which came a tremendous reduction in fatalities from many viral diseases.

With these successes in endemic and vector-borne diseases, the emphasis in medicine shifted from prevention to cure. Although many diseases could and were being prevented, and although large segments of the population were being protected from these large-scale afflictions, there are more than enough maladies to go around, and people kept getting sick on an individual basis. Doctors shifted to working on curing people one at a time.

This was the golden age for doctors. They were healers of the sick, curers of illness. To be sure, a new surgical technique or a new course of antibiotic therapy did not save hundreds of thousands, but they did help thousands or even tens of thousands, and that is no mean feat. People got sick and went to the hospital as in the past, but more and more often they did not die there, but got better and come out alive and well due in large part to the treatment they received there.

About twenty-five years ago, however, the cure model began to peak. While most patients got better, some did not. Some were not cured. For almost two hundred years the patient's expectancy curve and the physician's success curve had continued upward. But all the easy things had been done. People continued to get sick and die from the really intractable conditions like cancer and heart disease. The physician's success curve began to flatten out, and so good medical practice changed.

This change reminded me of a guy I was appointed to defend. He was a nice fellow who, unfortunately, had larceny in his heart. He was a con man who had been doing well with a scam involving a lot people, but his chickens finally came home to roost. The prosecutor would not plea bargain because of this guy's record, the defendant thought he could charm the jury, and I wanted some trial experience, so the case went to trial.

In listening to the testimony of the state's witnesses I was amazed at how he had been able to string them along, and I wondered why their suspicions were never aroused. After the jury was sent out for their deliberations, I asked him about this. He said that in running a successful scam people often become suspicious and when they do you have to say something that makes them feel bad about themselves. This puts them off, makes them uneasy, and most importantly distracts them from thinking about what you are doing.

In looking at health issues, I have begun to see that he knew what he was talking about. It occurred to me when I read about couple of studies dealing with pregnant women. One study found that as the number of prenatal visits rose, there was a one-to-one improvement in virtually every criteria by which we measure successful pregnancies—birth weight, head size, Apgar scores, etc. Women who had two prenatal visits did better than those who only had one, and those who had seven did better than those who had six. The optimum number was about eleven or twelve, because more than that indicated a problem pregnancy. The most important aspect of this study was that it showed us a real bargain in health care. A dozen prenatal visits are cheap, about $700 to $900, and the benefits are enormous—healthy babies, bigger brains, reduced neonatal care expenses.

The other study looked at drinking, smoking, and drug use by pregnant women and found that each of these can have a bad effect on the child in utero. This study documented that even in small amounts this use could be harmful, but doctors have been telling women not to drink or smoke for years.

Both of these studies were sufficient basis for making some public health policy decisions, so what did Dr. Everett Koop, the U.S. Surgeon General, and his successor, Dr. Antonia Novella, decide to do? They buried the one, and began warning us about the other.

This epitomizes the current state of medicine. Instead of health care, we get health warnings.

The Law of Large Numbers

Our health insurance system is a joke, if not a fraud.

Suppose a young engineer starts out working for a manufacturer, and he participates in its health insurance program with Company A. Let's also suppose that with the manufacturing business and all its problems, he develops an ulcer. If he changes jobs, our engineer can get health insurance at his new job, but the health insurance program with Company B will not cover him for the ulcer because it is a pre-existing condition. At first glance, this does not seem unreasonable.

Insurance rates are, after all, based on the idea that not everyone gets sick at the same time, so premiums build a surplus. If someone joins a group medical plan with a pre-existing condition, the company may have to pay for this person's expenses during his unhealthy period although it never had the chance to build a surplus by getting premiums from him during his healthy period. To that extent, allowing Company B to deny coverage for a pre-existing condition seems justified and not unfair.

But what about the former insurance company, Company A? If our engineer and his ulcer had stayed with them, they would have had to pay for the full cost of his treatment until the ulcer was cured. His going with the Company B means a net savings, a windfall, for Company A.

From an actuarial standpoint, the denial of coverage for pre-existing conditions of an employee who leaves one health insurer to go to another health insurance company because of a change in employment is a hoax.

The whole idea of insurance is based on the law of averages, or perhaps more accurately, the law of large numbers, which holds that over time and with large numbers everything will equal out. A health insurer may have to pay some pre-existing conditions, but will be relieved from paying for others as employees move from one employer to another. It will all average out.

Although a statistician might quibble with my definition, the law of large numbers says that the larger the number of the sample, the more likely things will average out.

If health insurance becomes more efficient as the numbers grow larger, then what is the best number? Obviously, the largest number—all. The best and most efficient health insurance system means universal coverage, the largest number possible. Anything other than a single-payer system with universal coverage is inefficient.

Sports Medicine

"A Puritan," according to Ambrose Bierce, "is a person who lives in mortal fear that someone, somewhere, is having a good time." It is not enough for the Puritan to live a good life; everyone else must toe the mark, and of course he is the one drawing the mark.

This definition occurred to me a few weeks ago when I

got a couple of magazines in the mail. One was a doctor's magazine for which I wrote an article, and I am still on the mailing list. The other was a legal periodical about workmen's compensation cases.

The doctor's magazine had an article about sports medicine. Treating people who have hurt themselves while engaging in some sports activity is becoming a new medical specialty because of the specialized injuries. While sprains and joint injuries are common, baseball players have a tendency to fracture the hamate bone in the wrist, and football players tear the menisci, the tissue that holds the knee together.

The workmen's compensation periodical was about the costs related to company sports activities. Some companies promote exercise and fitness by sponsoring employee teams or having workout rooms on the company premises. When employees injure themselves, by falling off the treadmill for example, these injuries are regarded as compensable injuries in many states. According to this article, in 1989 these employee fitness injuries cost 72 million dollars in workmen's compensation benefits nationwide.

Assuming this to be true, I began to wonder about the cost involved with fitness injuries that are not covered by workmen's compensation but by ordinary health insurance. It must be enormous, and I began to wonder if there was now going to be a great outcry against the fitness people. No matter what you do, you always gets this holier-than-thou argument, "Your lifestyle increases my insurance costs."

Some people are too fat; some sedentary. Others eat a diet of only what tastes good, and still others smoke or drink. All of them are continually flogged for not living the approved lifestyle. The problem, as I see it, is essentially one of tolerance and puritanism. Health insurance is the newtime religion.

We have learned religious tolerance after hundreds of years of burning heretics and scarlet letters and so forth. How a person views God and the world is pretty much his or her own business. We have learned that different beliefs lead to different practices and that we should tolerate people who do not believe or act as we do. But Puritanism dies hard.

This Puritanical strain has distorted our social accounting because for society, just as for the individual, there is no free lunch. If employee fitness programs lead to injuries, then we all pay higher insurance rates. But in the minds of the workers who pull their hamstrings and break their ankles, and their employers who pay for this carnage, the benefits outweigh the costs. The cost of having fitness people is a cost we all must bear. But because they enjoy exercise, life is better. Better for those who do, and better for those don't, because only in a free society one can make his or her own choice about how to live. Not everyone tries to fit, of course, but they don't have to. One is free to lead a sedentary life, hunched for hours over a chessboard, or slumped in an easy chair reading. To some the mind is more important than the body.

In my work I see the terrible cost of alcohol—about 60

percent of crimes are committed while the defendant was drunk. But for the average guy who comes home from work and has a couple of beers, or the couple who has a nice bottle of wine when dining out, life is a little better.

The argument that your lifestyle raises my insurance is invalid. While it sounds good at first, it fails to consider the basic principle of insurance—risk varies from person to person, but every person is at risk for something. By pooling the risks, and pooling the insurance premiums, we have a pool of money to reduce the loss in any particular case and even things out.

What you enjoy raises my premiums, but that's okay because what I enjoy raises yours. Life is full of things to be enjoyed—books, marathons, chess, basketball games— each with its own risk. But let's face it, the Puritans are never going to be satisfied and the insurance companies are never going to lower the rates.

Pain

The body's pain mechanism is an especially effective way of keeping us healthy. It sends us messages that say, like your mother used to, "Don't do that." So when you ignore the pain like you ignored your mother, and something bad happens, it tells you in that same maternal voice, "See, I told you so," and takes away some privilege. When you have a sore muscle, the pain mechanism is sending you a message telling you to go easy and give this muscle a rest. If you ignore this muscle pain message, it will go into spasm and you won't be able to use that muscle for a week or so. The pain mechanism gives us a lot of commands. Stop. Sit down. Take your hand off that stove. Sometimes the pain says to go see a doctor, and it even has messages for him. When he starts poking and prodding and asking does this hurt, the pain mechanism tells him, "No, No, No," and then "Yes!" When he pokes one more time a bit harder to confirm his suspicions, the pain mechanism says, "Yes, goddammit"!

Diagnosticians welcome pain because it is such a handy tool for locating and diagnosing the condition. People may be less than honest when talking about their eating habits, and will often lie outright when questioned about their sexual activities, but it is hard to fake it when something really hurts. When a person is wheeled into an ER writhing in agony, it may be angina, a kidney stone, an obstructed bowel, or a dozen other things, but no matter how bad it hurts the ER people will not give the patient anything for the pain until they are sure what the problem is. For some guy who is on his twelfth kidney stone and knows all the symptoms, and who knows that the only thing that will make any difference is a shot of morphine and atropine, the fooling around with x-rays and such is almost intolerable.

Wonderful as the pain mechanism is, doctors cannot seem to understand that once the diagnosis is made, pain serves no useful function. Since the body's ability to produce pain is far in excess of what is needed for a diagnosis, you would think that upon diagnosing a patient writhing in agony, the doctor would immediately prescribe large doses of pain killers. Not with the DEA looking over his shoulder. Even if the pain is indicative of an incurable illness, the DEA and life at-any-cost people will snatch the doctor's license if he overprescribes. Like the baited bear, the real danger is that patient might enjoy the relief morphine or heroin brings. Such is the state of medical practice today.

A Case History

I don't know if they still have high school students read O. Henry short stories anymore. Probably not, because the "in" thing in modern short story writing is all this minimalist drivel that passes for fiction. It's too bad because O. Henry is one of the better writers and his Christmas story, *The Gift of the Magi*, was one of his best. It is a simple story about a young married couple who are deeply in love, but are dirt poor. Between the two of them, they have only two things that they treasure. He has a beautiful pocket watch, and her pride and joy is her lovely blonde hair. With Christmas coming and with no money to buy a gift for her husband, the woman cuts her hair and sells it buy a fob for her husband's watch only to find, in an ironic twist for which O. Henry was famous, that he had sold the watch to buy a set of combs and brushes for her lovely hair.

That story is almost a hundred years old now, but I was reminded of it recently when I was doing some research on the issue of death and dying. A doctor told me a story about a man, a patient of his for years, that was almost as poignant. This man grew up in the Depression, and when he was fourteen, his father died leaving the family destitute. He dropped out of high school at age fifteen to help support his mother and youn ger siblings. He worked hard all his life, always had a second part-time job, and often worked two full-time jobs. He married, had three children, and was able to buy a small house. He put each of the three children through college, and even paid for one to go to graduate school. Considering his lack of education and the fact that he never held a really good paying job, this was a remarkable tale of sacrifice and hard work.

As the man grew old, he saw the doctor more frequently and the two became close. Life being what it is, the day came when the doctor had to have that terrible conversation with him—telling him that he had a terminal illness and that he did not have a lot of time left. The man took the news with equanimity. He told the doctor he suspected as much, that his life had not been so good since his wife had died three years before, and that he was proud of his children and what he had accomplished by his life of hard work. He could face death because he had accomplished most of his goals.

Then he told the doctor of one very important goal. His father's death and the resulting poverty convinced him that one of the most important things for a man to do was to leave something for children. He confided in the doctor and told him that over the years he had saved and invested and had a nest egg of $160,000 in CDs and conservative mutual funds. The doctor was in awe of the patience and discipline it would have to take for a man like him to accumulate that much money. He had scrimped and saved, denied himself a lot of things, but was very proud of being able to make this gift to his children. This was his final life's goal, and he had met that.

The diagnosis was correct and not too long after that he succumbed to the ravages of his disease and was hospitalized in the intensive care unit. His children rushed to his side. They insisted that everything that could be done, be done for their father. And it was. He had the tubes, the wires, the machines—the entire panoply of medical technology. Although the old man lapsed into a coma, one of them was always at his bedside. They loved that old man, and they knew how hard he had worked, how much he had done for them. The doctor suggested that there really was no hope and that perhaps less invasive procedures should be followed. As gently as he could, he said that maybe they should consider having a Do Not Resuscitate order put on his chart. They would not hear of it, would not consider anything that even hinted that this fight against death was futile.

But after several weeks, in spite of everything that was done for him and to him, the man died. The hospital bill for his final illness came to just over $147,000. The man had sacrificed for a lifetime so that he would be able to leave his children some money, because he loved them. They spent almost all of it in the last few weeks of his life in a vain attempt because they loved him.

Medicare provides health care for our older citizens, and

there is one amazing statistic about Medicare. Two-thirds of the money spent on most patients is spent in the last year of their lives. The average man or woman goes on Medicare at age sixty-five and dies about ten years later. One third of his or her entire cost is spent in the first nine years, and the other two-thirds in the tenth year. Why the enomormous increase in that last year? As a society we do what those loving children did in the story I just recounted. We spend billions to delay the inevitable death, while we cannot find enough money for ten or twelve prenatal visits.

That's health care in America.

CHAPTER 7

Physics

The Third Law of Thermodynamics

Those readers who are scientifically inclined are likely to say, "Hold on there! There is no third law of thermodynamics." Not so far, but that's why this book is such a bargain. I am going to tell you the third law of thermodynamics, and keep in mind you heard it here first.

For those readers who only have a vague idea about the laws of thermodynamics, a little remediation is in order. While you might not be able to state these laws in so many words, you do in fact know and understand them.

The first law of thermodynamics says that while energy takes many forms, it is conserved; that is, it remains the same. Suppose you have a certain amount of electrical energy. With that electrical energy you can run a compressor in your refrigerator, which will withdraw the heat from the interior of the box so the beer you have inside will get cold. Or you can use the electricity to fry a hamburger until it is hot enough to eat. The first law of thermodynamics merely says that even though you convert some of the electrical energy into mechanical energy, which cools beer, and some of it into radiant energy, which cooks hamburgers, the amount of energy remains the same. The first law of thermodynamics is not the problem.

The second law is. The second law of thermodynamics says that heat travels from the hot thing to the cold thing. To state the second law in ordinary terms is to say cold beer is always going to get too warm to drink and a warm hamburger is going to get too cold to eat. We can live with warm beer and cold hamburgers, but if we expand our example to the earth and the sun, you can see a difficulty.

The sun warms the earth in obedience to the second law of thermodynamics as its heat radiates out to us, but the sun is getting colder. Not only that, it is going to keep on getting colder and colder. Indeed, virtually every one of the billions of stars are also getting colder, and will continue until everything is just one uniform temperature. The ultimate reality of the second law is that eventually there will be no cold beer, no warm food, and no us.

To be sure, this is a long way off but the third law creates problems for us even now.

Another way of expressing the second law of thermodynamics is to say that ordered systems deteriorate. In a well-ordered world, beer is cold and hamburgers are hot, but one sees how soon that order deteriorates. Everything gets old, wears out, falls apart, or dies. What a bummer.

This tendency toward disorder is universal. You can impose order on a teenager's room, but it doesn't last long and soon the order deteriorates. Once you get the kid off to college, thank God, you can reimpose order on the room, but the deterioration is only slowed. Dust bunnies will gather under the bed, and the sun will fade the curtains. Disorder is the natural state of things.

Physicists will tell you that the second law of thermodynamics can be demonstrated mathematically, but there is a problem with that. The fact is that the more mathematics you know, the more unable you are to think clearly. Ask yourself this question. Don't you really think, deep down in your heart of hearts, that minus two times minus two ought to equal minus four? Sure, when the math quiz came around, you wrote in plus four as the correct answer so you could pass and get out of math class forever, but you never really believed it, did you? Me neither. This is the kind of thinking that leads a guy who has maxed out his credit card at $2,000 to get another one and max it out so that he is now twice as far in debt, to think he is "plus four."

There are some who do think this way, of course. We call them mathematicians. You hear stories about child molesters and drug dealers hanging around schoolyards attempting to seduce young children, but you never hear about mathematicians doing the very same thing in the classroom itself. Fortunately you and I have avoided youthful dabbling in drugs, sex, and mathematics, and are thus better able to understand the second law.

While mathematics is not of much use in understanding

the second law of thermodynamics, numbers are. When you speak of ordered states, nothing is so ordered as a set of numbers arranged in an orderly sequence. Take the ping-pong balls the lottery uses as a example. They start with a rack of balls all neatly arranged and numbered 1 through 50. Then they dump all the balls into a big plastic bubble with air blowing in it. When the balls hit the air currents, they bounce around and become all mixed up. Eventually, some of the balls get drafted up into a chute, and when six of them are there, you have the winning numbers. What are the odds of those six balls coming out 1, 2, 3, 4, 5, and 6? Astronomical! What are the odds, if you left the machine running, of all the balls coming out in exact numerical order? Insert your own adjective here.

When you buy a lottery ticket, you do not pick numbers 1 through 6. You probably use something like the kids' birthdays, like 7, 8, 10, 13, 22, and 26, or let the lottery machine pick some random numbers like 4, 5, 9, 10, 26, and 27. Yet the odds for those numbers are no different than for 1, 2, 3, 4, 5, and 6. You say you don't know the second law of thermodynamics, but you don't bet on ordered states, not in this world anyway.

The second law of thermodynamics is the strongest argument the creationists have. If ordered states become disordered, if everything is becoming more disordered, how can there be evolution where ordered systems evolve to become even more ordered? The frog is more complex than the paramecium. The monkey is more complex than the frog. We are more complex than the monkey.

To give you an idea of how complex we are, consider the guys who invented Viagra. This was a group of really brilliant scientists who wanted to win a Nobel prize. They asked themselves: What would a bunch of old men in Sweden think was a marvelous advancement in medical science? The answer: A pill that gives you an erection hard enough to hang a towel on.

As a sideline to their discovery of Viagra, this group discovered why blood vessels expand and contract, a question that had baffled doctors for centuries. Blood vessels, both arteries and veins, expand and dilate, but the amazing thing is that they do this depending on the need for blood. What the group discovered is that the expansion and contraction of blood vessels is controlled by the level of nitric oxide in the blood itself. When you are doing heavy work, the blood flow increases to your biceps, abs, and pecs. When you break for lunch, the arteries and veins to the biceps contract and the ones in your intestines dilate to increase the flow of blood for digestion. This is, by anyone's definition, an ordered system. It is like having a pipeline from Texas which, when it sends natural gas to Chicago, is twenty-four inches in diameter but becomes eight inches in diameter when it sends gasoline to Atlanta.

We are a more ordered system than the one-celled animal that first appeared in the primordial soup. And even that one-celled animal is more ordered than the strings of chemicals that floated there. A scientist in Australia did a real Frankenstein experiment—"It's alive!" He took what he thought was a bath similar to the primordial soup and zapped it with electricity to simulate the effects of lightning strikes. He said that with enough zaps, some of the complex molecules bonded together to form something close to the first one-celled animal. Now we have to wait fifty billion years to see if it will evolve into something like us.

What are the odds? In the previous pages, I asked you to use your own adjective to describe the odds of all fifty lottery balls coming out in exact numerical order. Now I ask you, what are the odds that a one-celled animal will evolve into a being so complex that its circulation system can read nitric oxide levels in the blood so that the blood vessels expand and contract as needed so that some scientists can win can the Nobel prize so that old men can get hard-ons again?

Viagra gives us a clue as to the third law thermodynamics.

Ordered systems become disordered, things wear out, men grow old, but sometimes there is Viagra. Some people do win the lottery. The six balls pop out randomly, a disordered state mathematically no different than any other combination of six balls. But what if they are your six balls? Winning the lottery is the most ordered of states. Sometimes the beer is really cold. We live in world overwhelmed by the whiners of the second law. Gloom and doom. Avoid this; don't enjoy that. Life's a bitch and then you die.

We need a third law of thermodynamics, so here it is.

THE THIRD LAW OF THERMODYNAMICS:
Yeah, but sometimes you get lucky.

A Brief History of Funding for Physics

> *"...a machine that is powerful enough to accelerate particles to grand unification energy would have to be as big as the Solar System— and would be unlikely to be funded in the present economic climate."*
>
> —Stephen W. Hawking,
> *A Brief History of Time*

In the early part of the last century, physicists made brilliant discoveries about the nature of the universe. The world was made up of atoms, which were made up of neutrons, protons, and electrons, all moving about in a well-organized and easily understandable fashion. There was symmetry for both the physicist and the layman. In the 1920s, however, physicists became dissatisfied because the current theories began to appear to be unworkable. "Unworkable" is a term of art, which has a precise meaning in physics: "We may all be out of a job." While the world was grateful to them for having discovered the secret of the universe, once the secret was out, what university would fund research for a physics department that already knew everything? The '20s were a time of crisis for physics.

But physicists as a group are a pretty bright lot and, applying themselves to this problem, made a marvelous discovery—the Heisenberg Uncertainty Principle. It was a godsend to modern physics. The Uncertainty Principle postulates that the examination of one characteristic of a particle, such as its velocity, affects another characteristic, such as its position. The two can never be measured simultaneously. It's like a half-inflated airbag. As one tries to wrap a tape measure around it, the mere pressure of the tape causes it to move and change shape.

The brilliance of the Uncertainty Principle as a tool for funding cannot be underestimated. Once any physics department can get funding for pushing down on the right side of the airbag, some other university must fund a program for pushing down on the left, or risk losing its reputation for being in the forefront of research. And, of course, when both research projects are completed, there will have to be a conference in some attractive spot like London or Acapulco to explain the discrepancy in results on right-side pushing and left-side pushing.

Einstein did not at all approve of the Uncertainty Principle. His objection gave rise to his second most famous quote, "God does not play dice with the Universe." That quote is taken out of context. When asked to comment about the nothing-left-to-discover crisis in physics, Einstein said, "God does not play dice with the Universe. He plays poker. If one would arrogate godlike qualities to physics research, one must learn to bluff."

Physicists learned to two cardinal elements of poker—never let people know what cards you hold, and continually raise the stakes.

Physicists went at these two criteria with a vengeance, and being brilliant people, came up with the ultimate in not letting people know what cards you hold. For example, in 1984, a physicist said, "For all physicists know apparently empty space is filled with particles that pop in and out of existence beyond their reach." This is the definitive bluff. One can't know what cards the physicists hold, since they admit that they don't know themselves!

I want to make a short digression here to say that I like physicists, who are as fine a group as one could meet. They are usually well-read, catholic in their interests, and often involved in community activities—just good all-around people to sit down and have a beer with. Chemists, by comparison, are dull or grim.

Chemists are dull because, working with nothing smaller than atoms or molecules, their entire professional careers are spent rearranging a few specific elements into some hope for combination. There's a lot of guesswork, experimenting, and computer models—what chemists refer to as "painstaking" research. Taking pains is dull. Chemists are grim because just about the time they have obtained their Ph.D.'s, they realize they are locked into a science that expects them to actually produce results.

Wistfully, they look at their brethren in particle physics. How nice it would be to deal with forces so obscure, particles so arcane, that they are posited on the grounds that they "ought" to be there. And all the while, the administration at the university does not even have the vaguest idea of what the physics department is doing. Nonetheless, the committee is absolutely convinced that they are dealing with the secret of the universe.

The budget process brings us to the second part of the bluff, continually raising the stakes. This is known in physics as quantum mechanics, from the Latin meaning "how much is this machine going to cost." Physicists know that no one will take one's work seriously, unless every year one asks for more expensive equipment. To the axiom that the world is made up of ever-smaller particles, they added a corollary: the price of the apparatus needed to examine a particle is inversely proportional to the size of the particle and its existence in time.

Physicists talk about things existing for nanoseconds. "Nano" is a combining form from the Greek work *nanos*, meaning dwarf, and is usually written as a billionth, or 10^{-9}. As a rule of thumb, budget requests from physics departments can usually be determined by simple mathematical inversion. Convert the exponent of the particle from negative to positive and add the dollar sign,

$$\text{Particle (P)} \times 10^{-9} = 10^{9} \times \$(\text{C}) \text{ Cost}$$

Nano-things are crucial in particle physics since they bring to mind the cliche, "dwarfs in comparison." The Super Collider, for example, dwarfs in comparison to the size and cost of any other scientific device. It will be fifty-nine miles in circumference, will cost \$4,400,000,000, and will, of course, help us discover the secret of the universe. Who could not want such a machine, nor the billions it will cost to build it? If one has four billion chips on the table, it doesn't matter what cards one holds in one's hand.

Not all is sweetness and light for physics. The chemists, particularly the biochemists who have been fooling around with DNA and helixes and such, are coming very close to trespassing on physics' turf. After all, in the minds of the average taxpayer the secret of life is not a whole lot different from the secret of the universe.

There is currently a great deal of interest in developing something spectacular. Yang and Mills did early work in this area in 1954 and came up with the gauge field theory, GFT, pronounced "gift." Hardly an appropriate name to get more funding. Norris and Bowman, even though their work languished unread in the journals, developed the idea of the Great Ultimate Fluxious Field, GUFF, pronounced "guff." While most physicists recognize the contribution of Norris and Bowman, GUFF was too close to the truth to be useful.

A breakthrough was finally made by Salam, Weinberg, and Glashow, who came up with the Grand Unified Theory, GUT, pronounced "gut." These men were true physicists of Nobelist quality. They didn't come up with a theory that would put everybody out of work again. Instead, they came up with an idea that makes a grand unified theory possible. When there is the possibility of such a theory, what budget committee wouldn't push dollars at physicists?

The Grand Unified Theory is a marvelous vehicle for funding. It sounds grand. In this age of mediocrity, where so few things can be called "grand," it is a delight to have a grand theory, like the Grand Canyon or Grand Opera. GUT is a wondrously appropriate acronym. A gut must be fed and carries with it the nuance of an insatiable maw.

The GUT deals with the elemental problem of physics, how to get more funding, by positing proton decay. Protons are, after all, the most stable, most basic particle. If protons decay, we are all doomed. To be sure, we are not doomed until 10^{33} years from now, but contemplating one's demise, even in the remote future, has a salutary effect on university budget admin istrators.

Administrators are tight. They feel it is their duty to husband scarce resources so that the university can continue to operate. At nonsexist universities, they husband-and-wife scarce resources. In any event, reckless abandon in spending is not in them, although the biochemists are working feverishly on discovering the markers for the spendthrift gene for transmogrification into their hard hearts. So far, administrators are still cheap, but when forced to contemplate the end of it all are less inclined to parsimony. Proton decay demonstrates that, ultimately, one should live by living for the moment, which by the way is 10^{17} moments since the Big Bang and 10^{64} moments away from the collapse of the universe. In the face of this inevitable implosion, keeping a jaundiced eye on spending is pure vanitas. Like residents of a plague-stricken city who realize the end is coming and it's only a matter of time, administrators can be convinced by the Grand Unification Theory to spend money today, so that as the universe comes crashing down on us we can know just exactly why and how it is happening.

Since the GUT is supposed to unify the four forces of the universe, but nonetheless has a demonstrable effect on purse strings, this effect is called the fifth force, or string physics. Very recently some people on the West Coast have suggested that there might even be a sixth force, but early test results indicate that this sixth force is insignificant even by particle physics standards—hardly more than the philosophy department's claim that they, too, hanker after the secret of the universe, and about as trivial as their budget requests.

But what of the future? The GUT, if successful, would put physics back at square one, back as it was in 1927 when Heisenberg arose like Lochinvar. Will history repeat itself? Probably not. Physics has learned a lot since then. A winner of the Nobel Prize for physics, Sheldon Glashow, has explained how close they are to ultimate knowledge, but then adds: "I don't think it will happen, but there's the exciting possibility that thirty years of work will go down the tube, and that everything we know now is totally wrong."

I would guess that it's more of a certainty than possibility. Physics and physicists have learned a lot in this century about physics and about funding. One example of their spectacular discoveries is the neutrino. A neutrino is a subatomic particle that has no mass, which means it is not matter, and it has no charge, which means it is not energy. If one asks what it is, physicists always dodge the question and start talking about angular momentum. One thing is very clear about neutrinos, however. If funding were provided to build an apparatus that could cause two neutrinos to bind together, and cause those two bond to four more, and so on until there were 2^{117} bonded neutrinos, physicists would have enough material to make the emperor a new suit of clothes.

Chapter 8

Environment

I n my old hometown I had a neighbor who was a Ph.D. in biology and taught at the university. He was a fine fellow, and like all people who teach at universities, was an expert on an obscure subject. His area of expertise was some small organism (I'm not sure whether it was a plant or an animal, but I think it was an animal) that grows in the cracks of grains of sand on many of the world's beaches.

At a neighborhood party, he told me that when he first began his study, the beaches of the Mediterranean Sea in southern France and northern Italy had grains of sand that were chock-full of these little critters. After only a few decades, he said, they had disappeared entirely from the Mediterranean, and he had to go to beaches in northern Scotland to find them. He was, of course, distressed by this.

His distress was caused in part by the fact that in the past whenever he was able to wangle some grant money to do field research, he could do it on the warm, well-fed, and wonderful Cote d'Or. Now he had to look for his little animalcule on some remote spit of land in cold, dreary Scotland. But he was genuinely distressed by the disappearance of many species, not just the one he had built his professional career around.

The disappearances of species was a big thing in those days—the major topic of gloom and doom. (Today, it is global warming, which we will talk about later.) The disappearance-of-species alarmists have lost some their vitality by reports that the world has gone through several periods where species of all sorts have disappeared. Some disappearances are understandable, like when the age of the dinosaurs ended with a large meteor striking the earth. Most other disappearances, like the trilobite at the end of the Sularian period, happened for reasons that seem unfathomable.

At the time of my talk with the biologist, the late '70s, these reports were not yet forthcoming so it was a good topic to bring up at the party. I said to him that perhaps things were not as dire as he anticipated. The cold war was in full swing then and the threat of thermonuclear annihilation was a real possibility. The nuclear nonproliferation treaty had not yet been signed by many nations, and there was real concern about regional nuclear wars. It was unlikely, I told him, that either the United States or the Russians would get us into a full scale shooting war and so decimate the earth. There was a real good chance that a couple of smaller countries, say Libya and the Netherlands, would get their hands on a few nukes and use them on each other. If all went well, these small countries could have their nuclear war without destroying all life on earth, but still release a goodly amount of radioactive material into the environment. This radioactivity would cause lots of mutations, and some of these mutated species would not only survive but prosper. While we were losing species at an alarming rate, we had the capacity to cause new ones.

He was not impressed with my idea. Scientists almost never are. But if the truth be known, we have the ability to create solutions to whatever problem we have the ability to create.

Global Warming

It's that way with global warming, the latest alarmist cause. Gloom and doom! It seems pretty clear that the world is warming, yet it is not all that clear as to what is causing it. Based on weather records of only a hundred years and core samples taken from glaciers less than 10,000 years old, some scientists are using computer models to project horrendous changes. The entire East Coast will be underwater, they say.

This doesn't bother me too much. Living as I do, at about 1,500 feet above sea level and 600 miles from the ocean, I am not all that troubled. While I would grieve for the people who were driven off their land, it wouldn't be so bad if I could drive to the ocean's shore in two hours instead of ten.

I take a longer view of things, particularly the greenhouse gas effect and amount of carbon dioxide in the atmosphere. Environmentalists are always going on about the changes to the ecosystem, but we ought to remember that the natural condition of the earth's atmosphere is CO_2, not oxygen. Awhile back, a long while back to be sure, the earth's atmosphere was mostly carbon dioxide. There was a period of great volcanic activity and in the smoke and dust put out by these volcanoes there were minute particles of ferrites, little bits of iron. As these bits fell to the earth they were absorbed into the oceans containing the very earliest forms of plant life, which just loved the stuff. They flourished and as all plants do when they grow, they consumed carbon dioxide and gave off oxygen.

This oxygen was the first air pollution—an adulteration of the pure carbon dioxide atmosphere of the earth. Because there was no EPA then, this oxygen pollution continued unabated for millennia until, as one might expect, there was an environmental catastrophe. The world's atmosphere became so saturated with oxygen that one day in the primordial soup where mutations occurred, a small organism crawled up on shore, took a whiff of oxygen, and decided that life was better on dry land. I am a direct descendant, as are you, of that little critter. When you hear someone talking about not interfering with the natural state of things, in all fairness you ought to assume he is in favor of greenhouse gases.

Only those people who call themselves environmentalists ever use the word pristine. Pristine this; pristine that. It comes from the Latin, *pristinus*, meaning from the earliest of time and untouched by man and hence, uncorrupted. *Mundus pristinus* was all CO_2. Do we really want a pristine world? That the world may be inexorably returning to its natural pristine state is bad enough; do we have to put up with a lot of holier-than-thou anthropomorphic guff from environmentalists telling us it's our fault?

Environmentalists

In Genesis God said, "Be fruitful and multiply, and fill the earth and subdue it; and have dominion over the fish of the sea and over the birds of the air and over every living thing that moves upon the earth." He also gave us every plant and tree, and passed judgment on His work by saying, "This is good."

This is not so good, say the environmentalists. It is too anthropomorphic to hold to the biblical world view. But the environmentalists are as anthropomorphic as anybody. The environment is the environment, and whether the atmosphere is mostly oxygen or mostly carbon dioxide makes no difference, environmentally speaking. All this talk about saving the environment is really just talking about saving us. If we live in an era of disappearing species, as we appear to do, our disappearance as a species would only be a natural part of the changes in the ecosystem, which has been exterminating species for eons. It may be our turn.

Even though this might be the most natural outcome, and even though the environmentalists claim to favor natural results, they still bitch about it. That's because that's what environmentalists do best—bitch. In terms of making policy choices or reaching decisions, they are virtually worthless. Consider their contribution to the debate on nuclear waste.

There is one spot in the United States that is better than any other spot for the disposal of nuclear waste. It is better because if you factor in all the variables—geology, physics, hydrology, economics, chemistry, meteorology, etc.—it is the safest, most efficient, and most practical place to put the stuff. Where is it? The environmentalists haven't a clue. I am not sure the government does either.

The government is excavating a great huge hole under a mountain in Nevada and wants to put all the nuclear nasties there. The environmentalists, and the Nevadans of course, are against this. You can check out their web sites and they will give you a dozen reasons why the Nevada site is no good. But that's all they do. They bitch about the Nevada site; they do not give any alternative sites.

There is a huge trench at the bottom of the Atlantic ocean, about five or six miles deep. We might throw our nuclear waste there, too. Again the environmentalists will tell you why this site is not good. Indeed they will tell you why virtually every site is no good. The one thing they will not tell you is where is that one spot in America that is better than all other places.

We have tons of the stuff now being stored on site, that is, at the various places where it is produced. It has to go somewhere. It seems to me that the environmentalists ought to be the group responsible for picking the site. Business wants the cheapest site. Politicians want the least politically damaging site. The environmentalists ought to be the ones to make an objective decision on the best site. The Friends of the Earth or the Sierra Club have as much data as anyone. Why not let them find that best of all places? Or better yet, let's pass a law that says that no environmentalist may speak out against any dump without being able to tell us of a better alternative.

I am not an environmentalist. It's not because I am not concerned about the world we live in, but rather because I have solutions, and to propose a solution to any environmental problem will get you drummed out of the movement.

Nuclear Solutions

I guess I am more pro-nuclear than most people. They tend to overlook its benefits and overemphasize it drawbacks. One major benefit of nuclear energy is that it is a constant cure for whatever current environmental problem we have. Twenty-five years ago when the major concern was declining species, nuclear radiation gave hope of mutations and new species. The current disaster scenario for the environmental Chicken Littles is global warming, whether caused by greenhouse gases or not, but here again, nuclear energy comes to our rescue. If we did do away with all fossil fuel burning power plants and replaced them with nuclear reactors it would do a lot to limit the greenhouse gases.

But if this is not adequate and it really does get too hot, we still have nuclear weapons. A little nuclear war between Libya and the Netherlands would throw a bit of radiation into the air, but maybe not enough. A nuclear war between Russia and the United States would likely throw up hundreds of millions of tons of dust and debris into the atmosphere and bring on the dreaded long-term nuclear winter. But if India and Pakistan went at it with their limited stockpiles of nuclear weapons we would very likely enjoy a nuclear cold snap. A few hundred million tons of debris thrown into the atmosphere will block out enough of the sun's heat to cool us down a bit. Simply put, a balanced nuclear war will return the balance of nature.

Nuclear and Solid Waste Disposal

But if we go completely nuclear, we will have a lot of nuclear waste, and I would be guilty of the very sin for which I denounce the environmentalists—unless I propose a solution to nuclear waste disposal. I will now do so, and as an extra added benefit—free, gratis, and for nothing—I will throw in a solution to our non-nuclear solid waste disposal problems. I propose the Logan County Solution.

The Logan County Solution involves two major considerations: the first being a reappraisal of our disposal techniques, and the second being the nature of Logan County itself.

Burying wastes and the detritus of society is very low-tech—hardly appropriate for a high-tech society such as ours. Before fire, all eating was done sort of takeout fashion, where you ate what you could at the site, took away whatever you could carry, and left the rest as garbage. As man developed fire, he also developed the idea of having dinner together around the fire; that is, waiting while the meat cooked and eating while it was still hot. After a couple of meals, the campsite started getting cluttered with bones and gristle, which drew flies. And so was born the garbage dump, a place out of the way where everything not being consumed was dumped. These dumps are the mother lode of anthropological science.

In the neolithic period, with the introduction of agriculture and herding, people became even more sedentary and produced even larger dumps. With history, civilization, and cities, the dump became even more critical to a successful society. The dump has been successful because in a low-tech society no matter what you buried, whether garbage or loved ones, would rot, decay, and eventually return to its essential chemical components. The sanitary landfill was, in fact, sanitary. Dumping was very effective because one could rely on the principle, "out of sight, out of mind."

High-tech societies are different. We make stuff that doesn't go away even after it is buried, like dioxin and nuclear waste. When you dump it; that is, bury it in the ground, it does not decompose but leaks and leaches into the soil and water. There is some debate about whether the Nevada site will leak, but it is a foolish debate. Of course it will leak in accord with Murphy's Law and the second law of thermodynamics. Thus, if we are to deal with the toxins of our high-tech world, we have to dump the dump. This is the first principle of the Logan County Solution—don't bury anything.

The second principle is the nature and location of Logan County itself. Logan County is a square in the center of Nebraska. It is twenty-five miles on each side, about 625 square miles. The South Loop River runs west to east through the southern third of the county, but it is mostly flat. It has only two major highways, one running north and south and the other running sort of east and west, through such little villages as Stapleton, Gandy, and Logan. With a total population of 900 people, Logan County is virtually uninhabited, and it has no bookstores where I might be invited to sign copies of my book.

The first step in the Logan County Solution is to make it entirely uninhabited. We would buy out all those living there and move them out. We should not be stingy, penurious, parsimonious, and above all else homophonophobic, niggardly about this. I would suggest paying $2,000 per acre and $1,000,000 per person to ease the pain of the Loganites; $800 million for the land and $900 million for the people may seem steep, but a mere $1.7 billion to solve our disposal problems is a bargain.

The next step in the Logan County Solution is to build a wall about eight feet high around the county and then to pave over the rest of it with about eight to ten inches of reinforced concrete. At the center there would be a special five-mile square, underlaid with about thirty inches of impermeable clay and covered with about eighteen inches of concrete, the nuclear zone.

This will be expensive. It will take about 500,000,000 yards of concrete, but the cost of pouring it will be reduced by building elevated train tracks so that the trains can just run over the trestles and drop the concrete on the fly. These elevated train track trestles are an integral part of the solution and will remain in place after the pour. After the concrete has set and there have been a few rainy days, engineers will calculate where and how the water runs off and build catch basins and impoundment reservoirs for treating the runoff.

When the building and paving are done, we will have a thirty-six square-mile nondumping ground. There will be twenty-five sections, each five miles square. In the center five-mile square, specially shielded trains will run over the trestles and discharge their nuclear waste from specially designed cars.

It would not, of course, be buried. It would stay right on the top of the ground where we could keep our eye on it. If the trestles were forty feet high, this would provide almost one hundred cubic feet of nuclear waste per person in the United States. More than ample. We could safely dump all sorts of stuff like short-lived low-level medical waste, twenty-nine-year half-life strontium 90, and even the really nasty stuff like uranium 234 with its 245,000-year half-life.

But what about radiation? That's the beauty of the Logan County Solution. Around our really hot center square are twenty-four solid waste squares. Radiation into the sky is not a problem, except that there would have to be a no-fly zone over the area. Radiation into the ground would be absorbed by good old Mother Earth. Sideward radiation would be absorbed by the miles and miles of solid waste surrounding it.

Just as the special trains would haul nuclear waste from all over the nation, regular trains would pull great huge loads of solid waste from New York and San Francisco to be dumped in Logan County. No city, no village, no hospital, no foundry, no laboratory—nobody—would have a solid waste disposal problem bigger than how to get it on the train bound for Logan. There would be no more NIMBYs and no more whining, sniveling environmentalists.

What would it cost? A lot if you think about the dollars that have to be spent. In dollars, the Logan County Solution will cost about 100 billion dollars. That works out to about $350 per person nationwide. A pittance if we think about how much we now spend every year, and a bargain when you realize it will stifle the Friends of the Earth and their ilk, who offer only complaints and no solutions.

Will this solve the problem forever? Maybe not, but with 100 cubic yards of nuclear waste capacity and 2,500 cubic yards of solid waste capacity for every man, woman, and child in the United States, it will go a long way.

And if we reach capacity, there's always McPherson County, population 600.

CHAPTER 9

The Economy

Free Markets

Free markets are more efficient than other human endeavors like governments, educational institutions, hospitals, etc. Let me explain why. Free markets are more efficient! Get it? No. Well, maybe I can explain it this way. *Free markets are more efficient!* Still don't get it? Well, that's probably because you're just another one of those people who typify the low level of understanding of economics in this country.

Perhaps we can raise that level by talking about economic efficiency. Free markets are more efficient because whatever the market does is efficient. In a free market, results do not matter. When Enron went down the tubes taking literally millions of people with it, and billions of their dollars, the Secretary of the Treasury told us that this is the beauty of capitalism; "Companies come and go."

Nonmarket institutions are not efficient because they

are judged by their results. If the roads are covered with eight inches of snow, or full of ruts and potholes, or bogged down in some monumental traffic snarl, it is easy to see the lack of government efficiency. If one out of ten people admitted to a hospital catch some sort of iatrogenic disease during their stay, you would not describe that hospital as efficient. Free markets may be efficient, but in all other areas of human endeavor success is a measure of accomplishments minus defeats.

When a company produces a useful and popular product and makes a lot of money doing so, the market is working effi ciently. When another company is mismanaged, makes an inferior product it can't sell, and goes broke, this, too, the economists say, is the market working efficiently to weed out bad companies. It is easy to understand why free market theory, whose cardinal principle is results-don't-matter, is so beloved by economists. If the free market is never wrong, then an economist who makes projections and economic forecasts about the free market can never be wrong either, just inaccurate. And if his prognostications are virtually worthless or even disastrous in making public or personal financial decisions, it's okay because the market, and the economist, are working.

Apply that same kind of results-don't-matter thinking to other human activities. It is not much consolation for a doctor to advise the family of the deceased, "The market trend is toward a boom in patient deaths." Imagine the sportscaster who tells his listeners, "Well, folks, it looks like the market is bullish on Detroit sacks." If you had twenty bucks on the Lions, you might not be satisfied with this standard of efficiency.

Courts are expected to do justice. To assess the efficiency of the courts, you would not look to how many pleadings were filed or trials held. You would look to the results to see if they are just. Justice is the goal; court action is the procedure. In the same way, free markets are only procedural. There is no question that in many areas free markets are efficient, but there are many problems not amenable to a market solution.

Take the example of the holdout, a classic example of game theory used to demonstrate nonmarket solutions. Suppose there is a shoal that is dangerous to coastal shipping. A lighthouse on shore near the shoal would be of great benefit, but the free market works against one being built.

Any individual boat owner could not undertake the cost of the lighthouse because it would put him at a cost disadvantage while benefitting the competition because, once built, it is there for all to see. The boat owners might form a group to build a lighthouse collectively, but from a free market standpoint, the optimum economic position for any single boat owner is to hold out. That is, to refuse to contribute in hopes that the others will build the lighthouse. The holdout is one of the main reasons we have government.

We have a government to do those things—schools, prisons, armies, roads, lighthouses—where the benefit is to all but which the free market, with its emphasis on the priority of the individual, cannot do.

There is no doubt that the free market is more efficient when it does free market things. But what about nonmarket problems and nonmarket solutions? Those who propose market solutions for every problem do not understand either the market or the government. Rep. Dick Armey, retiring after years in Congress, said, "Markets are rational. Governments are dumb." I believe Mr. Armey's long career in government is testament to that second sentence.

When you eat a jelly donut, if it doesn't taste good, there is probably something wrong with the donut. The market that brought you that donut is working fine, but the donut ain't. If the market is working fine while farmers are losing their farms and steelworkers are unemployed, then perhaps government intervention in the market may be warranted. I don't know why economists can't understand that simple principle. Let's look at some government intrusions into the market.

The Minimum Wage

I like the minimum wage. More precisely, what I really like is a proposal to increase the minimum wage—it has such a marvelous entertainment value. When there is no proposal to raise the minimum wage on the table, the attitude of economists toward the working poor is neglect, or perhaps in that wonderful phrase of Senator Patrick Moynahan, benign neglect. However, whenever a bill is introduced to raise the minimum wage the economists come out of the woodwork, dripping with sentiment

about the plight of the working poor, and tell us how raising the minimum wage will actually hurt the poor.

Raising the minimum wage will not really help the poor,
say these followers of the dismal science. To be sure, the
poor stiff may have a few extra bucks at the end of the
week and he may even think he is better off because of it.
But, the economists are sure to note, there is a real possibility that this increase in labor costs may make his job dis-
appear.

Of course, these economists do not have to do these
minimum-wage jobs themselves. They have learned the
first law of economics, which states, "There is more money
to be made in dealing with the problems of the rich than
in dealing with the problems of the poor." And one of the
major problems of the rich is having to pay poor people a
minimum wage.

Still, one must concede that there is some truth in what
they say. When labor costs go up, there is an incentive to
invent or produce a machine that will eliminate those
labor costs. These machines will eliminate many minimum-
wage jobs, and indeed they have.

But what kinds of jobs are eliminated? Dreadfully dull,
usually dirty, and almost always involving an unpleasant,
robotic-like routine. It is not a bad thing that these kinds of
jobs have been eliminated. The movie *Car Wash* was a
poignant portrayal of the people who did this kind of
work. It was kind of a working-poor ship of fools where
each of the characters exemplified a virtue, a vice, or a
value of ordinary people, but all who worked there were

numbed by the nature of the work. The boring, dirty, labor-intensive hand-washing of cars has now been replaced by drive-through automated machines because of raises in the minimum wage. There are very few hand car washes anymore, thanks (and "thanks" is the appropriate word) to the minimum wage.

A lot of other really nasty minimum-wage jobs like plucking chickens and washing dishes have been eliminated due to minimum-wage-driven mechanization. Only the economists regret this change. The typical minimum-wage worker, once he has been replaced by a machine, finds something else to do like running a machine that makes him more productive and better paid, yet the economists insist that he will sink into a life of welfare or marginal employment.

Welfare and Marginal Employment

There is a safety net to protect American workers from the vicissitudes of the economic cycle and other misfortunes in life, but the truth is we look down on people who get caught up in that net. Conservatives know that people on welfare are lazy, people on unemployment don't really want to find a job, and those on workmen's compensation usually fake an injury so they can draw a disability check.

In reply, organized labor and bleeding-heart liberals always offer the same old argument. They point out that most people are on welfare for less than two years, and almost always because of sickness in the family, divorce, or a substantial downturn in the local economy. When a breadwinner gets sick, a family gets hit with the double whammy of lower income and higher bills. When couples divorce, it's the same lower joint income and higher bills for separate apartments, utilities, etc. When a large plant in a small city closes, the workers can't find a job because the local competition goes up. They can't even move because with everyone out of work, a house is a drug on the market. So they end up on welfare.

The free-market economists, however, are too smart to be snookered by these arguments. They know that adding the social costs of production to a product or service increases cost of that product or service and thus makes our economy more expensive and less competitive. If you tack on to the regular cost of a product the added costs for unemployment, health care, workmen's compensation and pensions, the price of that product goes up. And the people who make that product are always in danger of becoming what the economists call the marginally employed.

But if they are right, one has to ask, how do those countries with much more generous benefits, like Germany or Sweden, not only survive but actually compete with us? The answer is that they understand the true purpose of the benefits and marginal employment.

Take the woman on welfare. No matter how good times are, she can't seem to find a job. She is a lazy malingerer and so is her live-in boyfriend, who is on unemployment. By God, we ought to force them to work. A few years ago, Congress decided to do just that by limiting the number of years one can get welfare and by insisting that she take a job, any job. In a similar vein, most states' unemployment systems have tightened up on eligibility or reduced benefits. And Social Security and workmen's compensation pooh-pooh any injury less than an amputation.

Anyone who has ever beaten the bushes during a down time in the economy might be tempted to think that most people are not working because they can't find a job. But let us suppose that the apostles of the Protestant work ethic are correct and admit that they are just lazy. What is having these people in the workforce likely to achieve? Do you want this lazy welfare queen to work in your office? Do you want her live-in boyfriend on your crew?

There are people, and you have worked with them, who are just workplace catastrophes. They don't do what needs to be done, and what they do do is so screwed up that it just makes more work for the other employees correcting their mistakes. And all the while they complain about how hard they have to work. You would be better off without them.

There's the secret. Sweden, Germany, and most other industrialized countries know that when you have a generous welfare scheme and liberal unemployment benefits the really lazy people stay out of the workplace. But how does that affect efficiency? It improves it. The hard-working Frenchman works hard while the French sluggard sits in the café and drinks coffee, and both are happy.

In America, it is the same way. Efficiency goes up on any day when the office jerk-off does not show up for work.

Lamentably, we in America insist that they do show up or starve, and our productivity suffers because of it.

If you have any questions about marginal employment, do this. When you go into work tomorrow, look around and see who in your workplace is one of the marginally employed. If it is you, slip on the floor and fake a back injury. You'll be doing your part to keep America competitive.

Welfare Queens

The public debate about welfare often raises the specter of the welfare queen. Nothing so outrages the ordinary citizen as the welfare queen who sits around and does nothing yet expects everything to be handed to her on a silver platter. Me, too!

For example, several years ago a man wrote to a newspaper tax advice column about his problem. He had inherited about $700,000 in the early 1980s. Not having an immediate need for the money, he put it into stocks so that in the early 1990s it was worth about $3,200,000. He wanted to know how to avoid paying any tax on his $2,500,000 capital gain.

Hold on here! What has this got to do with welfare queens, you are no doubt asking. The fact is—this rich guy, the capital gains king, and the welfare queen are two of a kind. Both expect to have it all without contributing anything in return. The welfare queen's unwillingness to do anything of value while still expecting to receive things of value is readily apparent to us, but when the capital gains king manifests the same kind of thinking, we don't see it.

The Capital Gains King

The capital gains king is a guy who benefits enormously from our societ, such as man doing so well that for over ten years he has never had to tap into his nest egg to get by. His investments have made money due in part to the global stability arising out of our large expenditure for an army and a navy. His business investment benefitted from a national transportation infrastructure of roads, railways, planes, and rivers. His companies had at their disposal an educated and trained worked force and access to the specialized knowledge developed and promulgated at many universities. He has never had to worry about cholera or plague, or civil unrest, and has always been able to rely on the police and fire department. Although some of his profits are in dollars that are worth less due to inflation, he still benefits from the stability brought to our monetary system by the Fed.

This went on for over ten years and his money more than quadrupled. Now when the time comes for him to cash in and take the profits from this period of stability, and he is asked to pony up a few bucks at the reduced capital gains rate, he balks. The capital gains king is the well-financed version of the welfare queen. He doesn't want to give anything back.

Surplus Capital

The major difference between the capital gains king and the welfare queen is that the king can hire economists, much the way Roman emperors hired auguries, to justify what they want to do, the old *bellum justum et pium*. The economists will examine the entrails of chickens, *statisticus*, and for a fee tell the capital gains king that he is a useful and, indeed, essential part of our economy. They will say that he should be applauded for providing the capital necessary for our economic growth and well-being, and they will conclude by telling him, and us, how wicked it is to tax this noble humanitarian and so confiscate his well-deserved rewards.

Notwithstanding the fact that economists' moral judgments are probably about as valid as their economic judgments, we ought to give the devil his due and think about the economic rationale that unless we reward investment, unless we generously compensate those who defer consumption in favor of savings, we will not have enough capital.

Maybe a no-capital-gains policy would be better, but what would the king have done differently? He had $700,000 to start with, but no current need for it, so he did not spend the money. What else could he do with it? He was not going to throw it away, so he had to put it somewhere where it would be safe. His choice could have been a bank, or T bills, or bonds, or the stock market, or whatever, but no matter where he put it, it would be part of the capital available and would earn some kind of a return. Simply put, all surplus is capital.

Economists tell us that interest is premium we pay to people who defer consumption in order to gather capital. Let's face it, people with capital do not defer spending on anything. As a matter of fact, many people without capital don't defer spending either, and they only stopped spending when they have maxed out all their credit cards and can't get new ones. The only people who defer spending in order to gather capital are the working poor and the middle class because they know they live in society that doesn't care much about them, their health, or their children's education.

When a young couple opens a savings account trying to get enough for a down payment on a house, we tax the interest on that account as ordinary income. When a fat cat cashes in on the money he really did not need to use, we tax him at the reduced capital gains rate, and then have to listen to him bitch about taxes. This is, economists assure us, sound tax policy.

Taxes

Let's go back to the lighthouse and imagine that it gets built. The issue now becomes how to pay for the cost of maintaining it and paying the lighthouse keeper. There is no question that since the boatowners are the primary beneficiaries, they should be taxed for the upkeep.

Imagine if the lighthouse government called a meeting to discuss the lighthouse tax. The owners of one boat would suggest a per-boat tax. An owner of ten boats would be in favor of a flat tax on all owners equally. As is always the case when tax issues are debated, things are likely to get heated and one can easily imagine the ten-boat guy saying, "That's stirring up class envy."

Class envy is the rallying cry today whenever someone suggests that rich people ought to pay more taxes than poor people. Class envy, as an argument, is a tautology, just another facet of the free market holdout problem.

I have here a quote from that progenitor of free market theory, Adam Smith. And because I have said at the beginning of the book that I would be applying the contemporary standards for research and authority, I want to emphasize that this is a real, exact quote, taken from *The Wealth of Nations*, The Modern Library, edited by Edwin Cannan, Random House, 1994, ISBN 0-679-42473-3. On page 888, the Father of Free Market theory begins in his section on taxes by saying: "The subjects of every state ought to contribute towards the support of the government, as nearly as possible, in proportion to their abilities; that is, in proportion to revenues which they enjoy under the protection of the state."

I would like to add here, parenthetically, that I have read a good deal of commentary from the free marketers about Adam Smith and the guiding hand and about government interference and a lot of other blather, but I have not once, never, heard an economist who said that Adam Smith favored proportionately higher taxes on the rich. Smith describes how tax policies can distort markets, but the economists never admit that for Adam Smith a tax policy that permits the rich to avoid taxes is a profound distortion of a true free market.

So here it is: Free markets depend on progressive tax rates.

In spite of all the maundering about free markets, we have adopted a tax policy that allows the rich to avoid their fair share, and you see where that has got us. The capital gains king spends his entire life amassing capital and avoiding taxes and as he faces death he realizes he cannot take it with him. His estate will be taxed. He goes to his grave still being the hold out, still objecting to paying his fair share. Give me the welfare queen any day.

Social Security

I know a guy, a young stockbroker, who is convinced there will be no Social Security for him when he retires. He will turn sixty-five in 2032, and Social Security is scheduled to go bankrupt in 2033. Because of this he is working hard to accumulate wealth so that come 2032, he will have sufficient assets to live on—and to live well—regardless of what happens to Social Security. By then he hopes to have over a million dollars in assets in today's dollars, about four to five million dollars.

I told him not to worry. Social security won't go broke. As a powerful white male politician, I know a little bit about how our government works. No one holding a seat in Congress would ever allow this to happen. If the Social Security system is in danger of collapse, Congress will enact a tax structure to dig up the money to fund the system. Where will the money come from? If there are only 1.7 working people for every retiree, obviously Congress can't get it from those still working because they won't have it.

Who will have it in 2032? Only those people like my stockbroker friend, who have been squirreling it away all these years. There will probably be fewer of those like him and many more who don't have a pot to piss in, and since we live in not only a capitalist society but also a democratic capitalist society, Congress will democratically, and republicanly, save Social Security from bankruptcy by adopting a confiscatory tax policy that will take the assets he has accumulated over a lifetime. He may not have his million-dollar nest egg, but, not to worry, he will get Social Security.

For those of you think that you can say to hell with Social Security, I'll get my own, you might be better off writing your congressman and demanding that the program be made both fiscally and accuarially sound.

The Lottery

Buying a lottery ticket every week should be a part of your sound investment program. Let me explain why. The goal of all of us is to be in that class of people called financially secure, and nothing so entitles you to membership in that class than to have a rich uncle who will some day kick off and leave you a pile of money.

Coming as I do from an Irish family, I have scads of uncles. My Uncle Mick was a caretaker on an estate owned by an American banker and was so gracious and charming you had to wonder whether he had found a job perfectly suited to his personality or grew into the job. My Uncle Mike was a brilliant electrical engineer who designed a component on the first satellite. My Uncle Padraic was a wonderful storyteller. I could go on for I had lots of really nice uncles, but the sad fact is, none of them came close to being included in the class of rich uncle such that I was never included in the class of nephew of a rich uncle who will kick off and leave me a pile of money.

Then came the lottery! Things changed. For a mere dollar, I could gain entry into that class of people who someday might have a pile of money dumped on them.

There is a lot of criticism of the lottery: "The lottery is a tax on people who are bad at arithmetic." The odds are so high and invite comparisons to being struck by lightning. But in truth, people do get struck by lightning.

I was out in the desert once, standing outside of a museum having a cigarette, when a woman security guard pulled up in an SUV. As she was backing into the spot reserved for security vehicles, I noticed her right front tire was going flat. I knocked on her window and told her about it, and as she got out of the car to look at the tire I saw she had a soft cast on her left ankle. She told me she had broken a bone in her foot as she hobbled around and bent down to look at the now almost completely flat tire. Then it began to rain. She was distressed about the whole business, but then she told me that the one event most likely to cause rain in the desert is a flat tire.

That's Murphy's Law. "The probability of any event is inversely proportional to its desirability," Murphy once said, and since winning the lottery is highly desirable, it must be just as highly improbable.

Perhaps no argument against the lottery is as invalid as the one that says instead of betting the lottery, you should put that two dollars into an investment for twenty-five years and see what you get. While not intending to conduct such an experiment, I actually did that. Starting about twenty-five years ago, I have bet two dollars on the kids' birthdays twice a week. At four dollars a week, or $200 a year, for twenty-five years that comes to about $5,000. I have never hit the big one, but I have won a few smaller prizes, so my net loss is about $4,700 to $4,800.

During this same twenty-five years, I was putting money into an IRA, a 401K, and some stocks. To date, I have lost $24,000 in the market, but one stock is particularly relevant. Like a lot of men, I had a small savings account that my wife did not know about. It was a small stash that I kept for bail money, loans to friends I didn't want to tell her about, and things like that. In 2000, it had reached about $4,800, and the market being in the frenzy it was, the stockbroker mentioned previously convinced me to buy some stock. It was an electric utility at $46 per share. It still is an electric utility except that it is now worth $3.18 a share.

Thus my net loss to the lottery is $4,700 and my net loss to squirreling away a few bucks is $4,282. To be honest, the lottery was more fun. Buying a lottery ticket every week ought to be part of your sound investment strategy. You can usually get them at the place where you buy your jelly donuts.

CHAPTER 10

Diversity on Campus

There is a need for diversity in our society, and thank God, some of our institutions, especially the universities, are doing all they can to promote it. When I went to college, it was all dead-white-male-Eurocentricism where the ideas of so-called Western Civilization were emphasized, and respect for the cultural values of other societies was denigrated. This narrow Eurocentric attitude was often disguised by such things as the hypocritical requirement that in order to graduate you had to take at least two years of a foreign language or pass a proficiency test in that language, but there was no requirement that you had to respect the culture or values of the people whose language you learned.

Today most universities have done away with the hypocrisy of the foreign language requirement, and stress the true value of multicultural diversity. This means that if you study poetry you don't have to read Frost, who was such a bad poet that he once said, "Writing poetry that

doesn't rhyme is like playing tennis with the net down."
Nor Donne, who is too long. In the interests of diversity
one should only read the poems of a Peruvian—a woman,
of course—and in translation.

Multiculturalists see the world as it actually is and not
through the distorted lens of Eurocentricism. Western
Civilization is afterall only a very small part of the entire
world and an historical anomaly. Eurocentricism arose by
mere chance after the introduction of such things as the
mold board plow in Renaissance Europe created a surplus
population that lead to European expansionism. This rapa-
cious expansionism lead to the attempt to impose on all
the rest of the world the values and methodologies of
Western Civilization. Eurocentricism imposed their
machines and instrumentalities, like the railroad, the water
pump, and the steel plow.

It really was an anomalous phenomenon where little,
tiny countries like Holland and England had control over
the vast areas of the sea and hegemony over vast land areas
like Indonesia, or the entire Indian subcontinent. But colo-
nialism and Eurocentricism has had its day, and it is now on
the way out. The forces that enabled it to achieve such
expansionism are deteriorating. For example, one of those
forces was the surplus European population. Today, the
population of Europe is declining. European nations are
not only not any getting bigger, they are actually declining.
It has been estimated that in a hundred years Germany will
only have half as many Germans as it now has. Italy's birth
rate is down, and it is expected to lose more than a quar-

ter of its population by 2050. In Spain, that one-quarter drop will happen only twenty five years from now.

To be sure Ireland is maintaining and even growing in size because with the improved economic climate, Ireland has forsaken its historic role as the supplier of brains and talent to the rest of the world through emigration. It would also appear that Irishmen, known throughout the world as inept lovers, can somehow still arrange to impregnate Irish women. This is a good thing, because the more Irishmen there are, the better off the world is.

The western half of Western Civilization, the United States and Canada, also have lower birth rates and are not replicating themselves, and they, too, would have decreasing populations were it not for a net gain due to immigration. That immigration is not European immigration, but from Asia, Latin America and, to some extent, from Africa.

It is on these three continents where most people live and all of them are nonwhite non-Europeans. You probably have heard it said that Islam is the largest growing religion in the world. This does not mean that people are converting to Islam in droves, but rather that Muslim women are knocking out babies at a rate of about four of five per woman. By comparison Spanish women reproduce at the rate of 1.07 per woman—a rate not even great enough to replicate themselves much less the present population of men and women.

Population is one factor, but not the only one indicating the decline of Western Civilization. The means of production have moved. It used to be that the non-European world was the supplier of raw materials and the Europe/North American world was the maker of goods. The Indians and Egyptians grew cotton, which was shipped to England, woven into cloth on the machines there, and sent back to be sold as finished products. Now there are industrial components in these countries and the monopoly is broken.

It is not unusual for academia to appreciate the changes in the world long before they appear to the ordinary person and therefore their grasp of the significance, and the promotion of, the trend toward multiculturalism and the decline of Eurocentricism ought to be applauded. Still, I can't help but wonder whether Western Civilization should be allowed to wither on the vine. All cultures have some value and a unique world view, even Eurocentricism's outlandish ideas about political democracy, free markets, sexual equality, universal education, and religious tolerance. It would be a tragedy if this culture were allowed to disintegrate in the sea of multiculturalism.

I realize that some people might say, "That's the way the world is." Societies grow and prosper and put forth ideas and a way of life, and when the world changes and the peoples of the world adopt more useful, more productive ways of doing things, those who cannot adapt fall by the wayside. This has happened in the past, and many peoples, languages, and societies have gone extinct. I don't think this should be allowed to happen to Eurocentric Western Civilization in this age of multiculturalism.

I know I should not eschew the cold, rational objectivity

that characterizes all that is written in this book but I will do so here in order to make an impassioned plea for the preservation of Eurocentricism. I have visited Eurocentric museums, and while I have to concede that they are woefully short on such things as baskets woven out of grass and beaded moccasins, they have created some interesting things like particle accelerators, spaceships, and foosball games. I have read some of these dead white male Eurocentrists like Hobbes, and Hume, and Rousseau, and they almost got it right—the stuff about living free and the ultimate dream of environmentalists, the state of nature.

While academia takes a long view, I take a longer view. I think we should act now in the interests of multiculturalism to preserve and protect Eurocentric Western Civilization. With a few simple changes we could do it easily. For example, while it is important that every college and university have a multicultural faculty and student body that reflects to the tenth of a percent the actual demographic makeup of our society, we could make an exception in a few cases. We could admit a few people who scored high on the SATs. To be sure, the SATs are biased, and academic achievement doesn't count much compared to a prospective student's racio-sexuo-ethno-homo-religio-nativo-cultural status. Still, we might try it.

Obviously we cannot disrupt an entire university for these few handfuls of Eurocentric throwbacks, but we might develop a special Eurocentric Studies Department. Because such a department would have only limited appeal to only a few students, we might have to institute some kind of affirmative action program, and we definitely would have to modify the usual standards for receiving a degree. Eurocentric Studies graduates would be required to know the history of their country and of the world. They would have to be able to read and write in English and have at least some fluency in another language. And, finally, like Eurocentric students of the past, they would have to know the names, if not the work, of at least one hundred dead white males.

There is a danger in creating a Eurocentric Studies Department given the penchant of Eurocentrists to criticize others and their performance. To prevent Eurocentric Studies from becoming remote, inaccessible baronies answerable only to themselves, we will have to adopt a multicultural loyalty oath and insist that every student entering the program swear to never, ever, pass judgment on anything.

"I DON'T KNOW WHY YOU MAKE SUCH A BIG THING ABOUT SHAKESPEARE. IT'S JUST A BUNCH OF OLD CLICHÉS."

CHAPTER 11

Politicians: The New Standard

I n the early stages of the first French Republic, as the parliament assembled, the conservative deputies tended to sit themselves on the left side of the chamber while the liberal deputies gathered together on the right. Frenchmen being what they are, and French politics being what they are, each side then began to antagonize the other side by sitting right down in the middle of the other's turf. Amid cries of "Point of order," and "You can't sit here," each side became so intent on pissing off their opponents that as a result all of the conservatives ended up on the right and all of the liberals ended up on the left. And this jargon of "right" for conservative and "left" for liberal has served as a useful shorthand for centuries.

In a simpler world, the left-right dichotomy worked pretty well because, much as neither side sat in the other's seats, neither the liberals nor the conservatives interfered with the other's ideological territory. The conservatives pushed for and defended fiscal and governmental restraint while the liberals wanted an open and more tolerant and egalitarian society. These conflicting ideals may raise questions about how money is to be raised and spent, or who the government should help or let alone, but these are not mutually exclusive goals.

Today everything has changed. The brightline distinction between what is right and what is left, what is liberal and what is conservative, has been blurred beyond all recognition. The free-market Republicans are spending billions on aid to farmers and putting import duties on foreign steel. The free-thinking Democrats are suppressing thought by enacting hate-crime statutes and adopting the *Plessy v. Ferguson* standard of separate but equal under Title IX.

This makes it hard on us politicians. I am a politician and have held political office for over twenty years. I am also a leading authority on local politics, because I wrote a book, *How to Win a Local Election*, and anyone who has written a book is, *ipso facto*, a leading authority. Everyone is well aware of the public's opinion of politicians, but are you aware of the politicians' opinion of the voting public?

At last month's conspiracy meeting, there was a discussion about the distressing trend in American politics where the politicians are losing faith in the voters. We politicians have a very low opinion of you voters because you lie to us. You say one thing when we are running for office, and then, after we are elected, you revert to the same old voter business as usual. For example, when Walter Mondale was running for president and when George Bush was running four years later, each man was asked about raising taxes.

George "Read My Lips" Bush said he would not raise taxes no matter what. Walter "Lost in a Landslide" Mondale said that he had no plans to raise taxes, but that if circumstances arose where it became necessary, he would consider it.

There are those who said that Bush won because he lied to the people and Mondale lost because he was honest, but they don't understand politics. George Bush did not lie to the people, the people lied to him. When he said no new taxes he was promising the people that he would cut back spending on such items as Medicare reimbursement for doctors, new weapons systems, cotton and sugar subsidies, and maintaining the Interstate system. Bush did not deliver on his promise to cut back but instead went right on providing these services to the American public because they really wanted them to continue.

When Bush announced that he would have to raise taxes to continue paying for them, the people turned on him with a vengeance. The seniors, the doctors, the arms industry, and the farmers all lied to George Bush. Implicit in their no new taxes demand was a promise that they would enthusiastically welcome and support a cut in the government program that benefitted them, but when push came to shove, they reneged and lied to Bush. He became George "One Term" Bush.

I am telling you, the voters, that you have to stop lying to us, the politicians. You tell us you want the government to stay out of private lives, but when one of us politicians has a honey on the side, you get all worked up. You proudly call the president the most powerful man on earth, but let's be honest. By definition, the most powerful man on earth can get a blow job when he wants. When President Clinton acted like a powerful man, all hell broke loose. In getting laid, there appears to be one standard for you voters and another for us politicians.

Just before every election you will see voters being interviewed on television, sometimes with their kids in the background to show they are good family people, talking about how they are interested in good government. Yadda, yadda, yadda. However, once a voter gets into the anonymous atmosphere of the voting booth, good government loses out to the narrow self-interest of the voter.

Perhaps the biggest failure of you voters is money. You have abandoned the political process to the big-money interests. It used to be that voters would read a newspaper, and not just at election time, and have some idea of what we politicians were doing while in office. Some voters would support a candidate by circulating a petition, putting up a yard sign, writing a letter to the editor, talking to neighbors, or even writing a small check to show where they stand. When we got some help in getting elected from voters, we spent more time talking to voters and rounding up that help.

Because you have abandoned us, we politicians have to spend all our time raising money to buy television time because you voters now get your information only from attack ads on TV. These ads may be sleazy, but that's because you voters are a sleazy group who pander your own self-indulgence.

We politicians try to do the best we can with such vot-ers as we have. We go to Washington or to the statehouse and try to work out a budget, or adopt a new policy, or make some kind of improvement in the lives of the people. And what do we get for our troubles? A lot of questions about "what's in it for me," and a lot more of "Screw the other guy, I got mine."

Still, we politicians have great faith in American democra-cy. We still believe that, deep down, you voters are basically good people. We look forward to the day when there is a better class of voters, more honest, less willing to sell out to self-interest. When you voters start to vote for something because it is good for the country regardless of whether it benefits you personally, or costs you personally, then we politicians will have that old-time respect for the voters.

CHAPTER 12

Animal Duties

Whenever I hear of animal rights, I ask myself: What are animal duties?

About a hundred years ago, a law professor at Yale named John Wesley Hohfeld wrote a wonderfully perceptive book called *Fundamental Legal Conceptions*. In it he noted that for every right there must be a correlative duty. For example, you cannot explain the right of one driver to proceed through an intersection on the green light, without discussing the duty of another driver to stop on red. Hohfeld pointed out that best way to describe any right is not in terms of what the holder of the right might do, but rather in terms of the duties that right imposes on others.

Hohfeld taught real property law and his book is full of property law examples, but even a nonlawyer can easily see the point he was making. The concept of ownership involves certain rights such as possession, but possession is best understood in terms of the duties it imposes on others. Possession by the owner is the right to have and use the property for oneself, but more importantly the duty of someone else to leave when the owner says, "Get the hell off my property."

There could be an enormous list of rights that are described in terms of the duties such as freedom of religion, or freedom from discrimination, but there is one area where the Hohfeldian analysis breaks down—animal duties.

About fifty years ago, the cartoonist Al Capp created the Schmoo. The Schmoo was a small chicken-like animal, without wings, but with an irrepressible desire to please people. If you needed eggs, the Schmoo would lay you a dozen neatly packed in a carton. The Schmoo would also lay butter and milk in bottles. More than that, the Schmoo would gladly roll over and die when needed for a roast Schmoo dinner. The Schmoo was the ultimate in domesticated animal.

Vegetarians would be appalled by the Schmoo. They condemn animal husbandry (or animal husbandry and wifery; see chapter 13) as slavery and murder and those of us who eat chicken or wear leather belts as slavers and murderers. Vigorous as they are in their proselytization, they appear to have never given a thought as to what might occur if they succeed in converting the rest of us. If we all become vegetarians, what will happen to the cows and the chickens? As it is now, they are two of the world's major species and nowhere near getting a place on the endangered species list, but who in God's name would keep a cow or a chicken except for the milk, eggs, meat, and leather. If we didn't eat their eggs, hens would be as rare as hen's teeth.

One of the problems for traditional evolutionary theory, which posited the idea of survival of the fittest, was the fact that many animals engage in selfless behavior. If he is interested in his own survival, what would induce the worker bee to go out and kill himself to protect the hive from an attacker or honey thief? Modern evolution theory has come with the idea that it is not survival of the individual, but survival of the species that compels behavior.

The ants and aphids, the sharks and pilot fish, the humans and cows, are all good examples of a symbiotic relation that benefits both species. Wearing fur is offensive, but the unfortunate truth is that minks, stoats, and sables are nasty animals, and indeed there is almost a one-to-one correlation between the viciousness of an animal and the softness of its fur, and because of this these species prosper. The absolutist animal rights types are not a group given to deep thought, but they probably have at least enough sense to realize that if they eliminate minks being killed, they will also eliminate minks being born.

There has been an awful lot of talk about the deleterious effect of the expansion of the species Homo sapiens on other species, like wolves and tigers, who eat Homo sapiens. Evolutionarily speaking, eating Homo sapiens is not a good survival strategy. A much better strategy is to be a species that homo sapiens eats. In *Near a Thousand Tables*, a wonderfully incisive book, the author suggests that one might reasonably look at the history of the world as the expansion of the wheat species, using man as aphids, to establish itself as the world's predominant species. The best survival strategy, of course, is to be involved with Homo sapiens' sexual habits like crabs, venereal wart fungus, and those lesser animals, the herpes and AIDS viruses. So what are the animal rights activists most likely to accomplish? The destruction of a lot of species not now threatened.

So what are the animal rights people really after? They want to be better than you, to be holier-than-thou. They want to do good, but doing good too often runs aground, as do-gooders have found, on the shoal of ingratitude. Those who do good for other people often find that the do-goodees are unappreciative or even resentful of the good being done to them. People for whom good is being done complain and whine that it is not enough or even that it is not what they need.

How much nicer it is to do good for dumb animals, who being dumb, never complain to the do-gooders. Whales, they say, can communicate with each other, and one can easily imagine Freed Willy reunited with his family around the feeding ground.

When his brother asks, "Where you been?" Freed Willy would say, "I had this incredible gig. The quarters were a bit small, but they kept them scrupulously clean. There was free medical, and the room service was awesome. All I had to do was roll over or jump out of water and they would throw me fish. Occasionally, not as often as I would wish, they would bring in a female so I could mate. The staff was so well-trained that they would throw you a fish whenever you waved your tail."

At this point, Freed Willy's sister-in-law would break in and say, "Willy, you shouldn't be filling the kids' heads with such nonsense about free fish. They have to learn that if you want to eat, you have to find your own fish. Children, don't believe everything your Uncle Willy says."

"So what happened?" asks his brother, and Willy, ungrateful wretch that he is, would describe his being freed as being evicted, starved, and abandoned. Fortunately, since humans cannot communicate with whales, the people who did good for Willy never have to hear his thoughtless spiel.

One of the criticisms brought against the animal rights activists is that it is unseemly or even unconscionable in a world filled with so much human suffering, with war, famine, and disease, to be more concerned about animals than people. That criticism fails to understand the two basic principles of the animal rights movement. Animals are nice. People are shits. Sometimes ungrateful shits, sometimes foolish shits, sometimes malevolent shits, but always shits.

Take for example the not-tested-on-animals campaign. The stories of poor bunny rabbits getting eye infections were so successful that cosmetic manufacturers now proudly print on the label that this product was not tested on animals. Which means, of course, that it is tested on people. The bunny rabbits are now spared while some preteen girl fooling around with mascara might go blind, but that's okay. She is, after all, only human.

The attitude of animal rightists towards their fellow human being is best exemplified by the cat vet at Ohio State University. For years he had been doing experiments using cats, working on understanding a retrovirus that significantly weakens the feline immune system. Sounds a bit like AIDS, doesn't it? Indeed. When the AIDS epidemic hit, a lot of human medical researchers found his work to be very helpful in understanding retroviruses and how they work. (By the way, the next time some congressman gets up to talk about waste in government and uses as an example an appropriation for basic research, ask him about the study of feline retro viruses.)

The cat vet was initially praised for the work he did with his experiments on cats, but now he is trouble with the animal rights people. What did he do to incur their wrath? He is testing the use of methamphetamine on cats to see if that might lead to a cure, or at least a treatment, for AIDS. After a lifetime of experimenting on cats to help cats, he is now trying to help *people*. The swine!

There is a dangerous aspect to this animal rights business that is often overlooked. Vegetarianism leads to political instability. I read one very interesting study that drew a one-to-one correlation between the degree of political stability in a society and their consumption of meat. The more meat consumed in any country, the more likely it was to have a stable society in terms of educational levels, health care, and reliable financial and political institutions. One critic of the study pointed out that maybe it wasn't the consumption of meat that led to stability but rather that as societies became more stable and more prosperous, they could afford to consume more meat. Perhaps, but I am using that study in accord with the principles of modern epidemiology. That is, when you have some sort of ax to grind, you cite a study to foreclose reasoned debate on an issue.

And look at the way the meatless animal rights people behave. They throw blood on models in fur coats and bomb laboratories. Animal rightists are like the anarchist bombers of yore or the terrorist bombers of today—the very epitome of violent, unstable political activity.

Thus, it would appear that everyone has a civic duty to consume meat because that consumption leads to a more stable society. I think most of us do our part. We scarf down hamburgers and steaks as we embrace the ancient virtue of *civitas*.

The animal rights people do make a good case for meat being produced on factory farms. Chickens raised in the hothouse environment of modern breeding farms are jammed into tiny cages and slaughtered after only six or seven weeks. As a result, they have no taste. Free range chickens taste better. If the PETA people were really interested in improving the lot of chickens, they would start a campaign for better-tasting chickens, and cows, and pigs. The fact is, however, they really don't give a damn about the animals. What they want is not to control animal production, but to control you. It's just one more example of "I don't like it, so you can't do it."

The difference between animal rights and human rights is that human rights revolve around duties; that is, duties to your fellow man. The moral imperative is clear. Animal rightists and other vegetarians have a moral duty to eat meat to promote stability and happiness in our society. Liberal that I am, I would not insist that the law require them to actually eat meat, but I would require all animal rightists to carry a card that reads:

> *My right to exercise any freedom depends almost entirely on my duty to allow that same freedom to others, and the extent of my freedom depends on the extent of freedom I am willing to grant to others in the exercise of theirs.*

Animal rights? Perhaps there ought to be animal rights, but if so, please describe them to me in terms of animal duties.

CHAPTER 13

Sexism in Language

A few years ago I wrote an article for a lawyers' magazine about writing a good brief. As a sideline to my judicial career I have spent many hours at legal writing seminars trying to teach lawyers how to write a simple declarative sentence. I have recommended that they join the support group for writers of legalese, On and On Anon. In the article, echoing Strunk and White, I urged the lawyers to avoid clutter. When the article came out the editors had, without consulting me, changed my every use of the third person personal pronouns "he" and "his," to "he or she" and "his and hers." This was the very sort of clutter I was against.

I had written, " A lawyer should always file his brief on time." I had also written, "A lawyer should make it a point to listen to what his or her client has to say." As published, it came out as "his or her brief" and "his or her client." I was trying to make a subtle distinction. In the first sentence I was speaking of lawyers in general, lawyers as a group of professionals. In the second sentence I was speaking to lawyers as people, real live human beings, people who often do not listen to their clients. This kind of precision is, I am now told, sexist.

I had the same kind of go-round with the reporter for the Ohio Supreme Court whose job it is to publish selected opinions. He did that to one of my opinions and when I objected he said it was now the policy of the court to use "gender-neutral" language. I suggested that the court either leave my opinions as they were or not publish them. A fat lot of good that did.

Every year I fill out the Supreme Court registration form for my license to practice law where they have a box that says "Gender: ❏ Male ❏ Female." To be precise, my sex is male and my gender is masculine, and there is a significant difference between gender and sex. Had any really hot gender lately? I always cross out Male and write in masculine, but they haven't revoked my license yet.

I have published over two hundred pieces, not counting opinions, and one other book. I have no pretensions about being a good writer, but I do have pretensions about trying to be a good writer, about trying to use the most precise word, and sometimes, when I look back on what I have written, including opinions, I think, "My God, did I write that?" Using the right word is a bit of a misnomer. The real trick is to use the best word, the one most likely to convey the idea in your head.

While doing an acrostic puzzle, I came across this line from Shakespeare's *Henry V*, ". . . the casques [arrows] that did _____ the air at Agincourt." I tried to think of a word. Fill? Charge? Saturate? Pervade? What word would convey the terror of the French as they stood under that deadly shower of long bow arrows. Shakespeare wrote, "The casques that did *affright* the air at Agincourt." Affright is probably the best word. That's a precise use of words.

About the only area left where precision in language is demanded is in describing the sexual practices of a woman. A woman might be loving, affectionate, friendly, warm, easy, loose, mistress, prostitute, whore, slut, cunt. Woe betide him who misuses a word on this sliding scale. For men, of course, there is only one word, horny.

Precision has been replaced by the use of words that are politically correct, and the banning of words that are not, but it's hard to know what words are no longer correct, and even harder to know why. Oriental is out. I'm not sure why. I am not sure, either, about occidental. I used to use occidental occasionally just to be pretentious, but stopped when I realized that people didn't know what I was talking about. (It means Western, the opposite of Oriental.)

In trying to find out what is now sexist I checked out a couple of stylebooks put out by the Associated Press and the *New York Times*. Stylebooks are desk manuals for journalists, used as a handy reference when writing copy. The stylebooks demand gender-neutral language. Actress is out. There is probably no more important criteria in assigning a dramatic role than the sex. There are parts for men and parts for women, and the times where an actor can pull off a crossover like Dustin Hoffman in *Tootsie* or Jack Lemmon and Tony Curtis in *Some Like It Hot* are regarded as an acting triumph. Julie Andrews did double duty playing a woman playing a man playing a woman. Actor is gender-neutral, but acting is not. Likewise, we have no more heroines. Only heroes. Except we don't have heroes either in the era of historical deconstruction.

Man is out, as in businessman, congressman, or spokesman. Oddly enough so is businesswoman, congresswoman, or spokeswoman. They have been replaced by persons, which is better than being replaced by an inanimate object, the chair. In the good old days there were few, if any, women who got to be chairman of any committee outside of a women's club. And if they did, they would be referred to as the woman chairman of the finance committee. Now we have a lot of women running a lot of committees and they are called "chairs." With all their talk about equality of opportunity and encouraging young women in nontraditional careers, you would think that the feminists would encourage the use of chairwoman and congresswoman. Indeed, it may be a male plot. Now that women are getting some of these responsible powerful white male jobs, our sexist society cannot face it and uses gender-neutral language to deprive congresswomen and chairwomen of their rightful recognition.

I am not against all of the changes made in the interest of political correctness because some have added to the precision in our language. Mail carrier is better than mailman and more accurately describes what mailmen do. Fireman used to mean one who started fires in boilers, but also meant one who put out fires in houses. The change to firefighter is more precise. Nor do I object to such generic words, like police officer where women are doing men's work. What I really object to is the inanity of gender-neutral policy as being thought of as good writing.

Way back in grammar school English class, you were taught that a pronoun must agree with its antecedent in gender and number. You were also taught that because English lacks all the pronouns it might have, when there is a problem the masculine form is preferred. This, we are now told, is sexist, but it really misunderstands how English works and how it got to be that way.

English is a hodgepodge language thrown together after the Norman invasion of England. The Normans, who spoke French, threw out all the Anglo-Saxon nobles, but kept the serfs who also spoke Anglo-Saxon. Thus, in English we have separate words for meat on the hoof—pig, cow, sheep—and meat on the table—porque, boeff, and mouton. The serfs continued to raise the animals and call them by their Anglo-Saxon names, while the lords who got to eat the meat used their language to describe the food.

English is thus a sort of pidgin English resulting from the Norman lords trying to talk to and get some work out of their Saxon serfs. On top of this, there were the clergy who spoke and, being the only ones who were literate, wrote in Latin. In spite of all the difficulty, they were able to cobble together a pretty good language which, as Shakespeare proved a few hundred years later, was both dynamic and precise.

What English lacked, however, was a lot of pronouns. We have first-person singular I, second-person you, and the third-person in masculine, feminine, and neuter—he, she, and it. What we don't have it a third person impersonal pronoun. So the grammarians have decided that agreement in number is more important than agreement in gender; thus, we should use "he." This is now sexist.

Gender neutralism posits a first principle that there is a correlation between the use of pronouns in a society and the status of women in that society. This principle might be acceptable if one were almost completely ignorant of other languages and societies. In Latin, the Romans gave women scads of feminine pronouns but also held to the doctrine of the *paterfamilias,* which gave the man absolute power, sometimes even the power of life and death, over the women in his family. French has long had equality among the sexes in pronouns, if not in real life in France. And Spanish, which grants women a high place in the pronominal hierarchy, is the language of machismo. Conversely, Chinese is absolutely gender-neutral with the third person "ti" as a pronoun that does it all, being masculine, feminine, neuter, impersonal, personal, possessive, and just about anything else you want. The Apache, "agon," does the same thing. Neither the Chinese nor the Apaches are known for their gentle treatment of women. All sexist English has ever given us is such things as the rights of *man*, and masculine preferred.

It is not just pronouns that come up short in English. We have many words that do double duty. We have round balls and balls with music. Effect usually means a result, but sometimes means to cause a result. And to complicate things, "affect" means to cause an effect, so everybody now says impact. I never use the word "impact" unless there is debris, broken glass, or bent metal involved.

Is it sexist to say a lawyer should file "his" brief on time? When all the men were lawyers, it was not sexist but accurate. Now that we have a lot of women lawyers, "his" may be less accurate, but is it sexist? It seems to me that it is discriminatory toward men. In English, if the antecedent is absolutely female, as in mother, you use "her." If the antecedent is absolutely male, as in father, you use "his," but if you don't know or if it is a mixture of male and female, you use "his."

Women have their own feminine pronouns and their use is exclusively reserved for them. Masculine pronouns, like a lot of other English words, do double duty. To some this is sexism in language. To me it is just a reflection of the status of the male in American society. Men, like the masculine pronoun, do twice the work for half the credit, and all the while the illiterate feminist harpies scream about how unfair life is.

"HOIST ON HIS OR HER OWN PETARD"

CHAPTER 14

Risk

The Head of the Messenger

Here is the true story.

"Alarm, warning," cried the messenger as he rushed into the King's bedroom. "The enemy has crossed the border at three points and is marching on us with an army of 50,000 men."

"My God," said the King, "Get the prime minister and the generals." He jumped out of bed and lit a cigarette.

"Alarm, warning," cried the messenger. "The royal surgeon has determined that smoking is dangerous to your health."

"Bring me some bacon and eggs," ordered the King, stubbing out the cigarette.

"Alarm, warning," cried the messenger. "Two eggs contain more than three times the daily allowance of cholesterol and bacon is full of nitrosamines, which lead to heart attacks or strokes."

"Bring me a bowl of cereal and some milk."

"Alarm, warning," cried the messenger. "Whole milk contains fat, which clogs the arteries, and processed cereal contains trace elements of pesticide residues."

"Get me a cup of coffee."

"Alarm, warning," cried the messenger. "The caffeine in coffee is known to have an adverse effect on . . ."

What caffeine is known to have an adverse effect on is unknown because at that moment the King pointed to the messenger and shouted, "Guards, off with his head!"

Americans today are like the King. We are inundated with warnings about this and the risk of that.

Methylcyclopentadienyl manganese tricarbonyl is a gasoline additive used to raise the octane level of the fuel. The EPA banned its use because it was concerned about the long-term effects of MMT, as it is called. The EPA did not know anything at all about its long-term effects and it admitted in court that there was no evidence of any adverse health effects, but it felt that MMT should not be used until they were sure it was safe.

As to risk involved with MMT, we might get fewer warnings if we were to adopt a rule that one may not use the initials of any compound in debating legal, environmental, or public policy questions; the debate would be much shorter. If the EPA bureaucrats and the environmentalists had to say "Meth-yl-cy-clo-pen-ta-di-en-yl-mang-anese-tri-car-bon-yl" over and over again, they might find it less risky.

The most typical aspect of the case against MMT, however, is the EPA spokesman's comment on risk. He told the *New York Times*, "There may be a threat here and no one has the data to say there isn't one." We are a society gone mad with the fear of any risk because that statement is considered sensible, even prudent. Implicit in the statement is that all new things are suspect and probably harmful. The "X" in generation X must stand for xenophobia.

Consider the opposite. Suppose someone promoted a government program and argued in support of it by saying, "There might be some benefit to this program, and no one has the data to say whether there is or there isn't, so we are going ahead with it." Without data either way, one presumption is as valid as the other. However, the public has been conditioned to think that risk, any risk, is dangerous, or even unthinkable.

There is no question that with all the inorganic and organic chemists knocking out new compounds every week, some of those compounds will have some effect on how we live and how we die. Some will have obvious beneficial effects and others will have obvious pernicious effects, but it is not the obvious effects that seem to bother us. Virtually every compound made will eventually work its way into the environment, often as a trace particle in parts per billion. That parts-per-billion stuff is a major part of our problem with risk. It used to be that chemists could only analyze parts per ten thousand or parts per hundred thousand, but now they can find some parts per million, parts per billion, and even with some substances, parts per trillion. This masterful advance in chemical technology, useful as it is, has its own risk. There is the risk of thinking that because some compounds are quantifiable in the smallest of amounts they must also be effective in those amounts.

Consider warfarin, a commonly used rat poison, which is particularly nasty stuff because of the way it works on rats. Rats are like people in a lot of ways, which is why they make good subjects for lab experiments. Rat's blood is like ours in that in contains clotting factors that prevent hemorrhaging, and warfarin works by destroying the clotting factors. When a rat eats warfarin, the clotting factors are destroyed and the poor rat bleeds into his own lungs until he suffocates and dies.

Cumidin, a medicine given to tens of thousands of people every day, is warfarin in very small doses. It is used to prevent the clots that cause strokes but it must be carefully monitored because too little won't work and too much has the same effect of warfarin. Is it risky? Sure, but life is a risk.

I used to ride a motorcycle and it was pretty risky. Not riding, but the jerks on the highway who seem unable to see motorcycles; they cut you off or pull out in front of you as if you were not there. Based on accident reports and comments from bikers, the jerks are still out there. Some riders wear helmets, and there is no doubt that these helmets limit the risk of death in a motorcycle accident. But wearing a helmet involves risk, too. A helmetless rider has a good chance of having his brains bashed out as he slams into some unmovable object at the side of the road. The rider with the helmet who hits the same object does not die because his head is protected. Instead, his spine takes the force of the blow and he is left para- or quadriplegic.

One should expect that the rider could decide for himself on which option is riskier, but people who would never ever get on bike insist that bikers wear helmets. These nonriders pass laws that require riders to embrace and adopt not only their perception of the risk, but also their perception of risk avoidance.

I would take a more balanced view. I would not require helmets, but I would mandate that they all carry organ donor cards. When the helmetless rider bashes his brains out, the rest of his organs are usually still in pretty good shape, and there is always a long line of people waiting for a new heart, liver, etc. This is called risk benefit analysis.

For every risk, there is usually some benefit. What behavior increases your chance of getting cancer more than any other? Growing old. Cancer is, mostly, a disease of old people and most people are willing to undertake that risk. But even at that, there the so-called preventable deaths.

A few years ago I read in the newspaper of the death of top-rated climber who died, along with several of her fellow climbers, as they descended K2, a notoriously treacherous mountain in the Himalayas. In a television interview before her death, she said she began climbing as a young girl and spoke of the exhilaration, the rush, that comes from being at the top of the mountain. I guess she also found it exhilarating to be at the top, not just of the mountain, but of the sport itself. Being the best at anything is pretty heady stuff. She was in her thirties, and had a husband and two small children, and I wondered why she would climb mountains. I am sure that climbing mountains took time away from her family, but parents who are determined to be the best often have to set priorities, and their children have to take them as they are. Still, to have risked her life this way, to have cost her children the love and comfort of their mother, seems vaguely irresponsible. I don't climb mountains because it is too risky.

As I sat reading of her death, cigarette in hand, it occurred to me that she probably did not smoke, and almost certainly did not smoke around her children. Most climbers do not, and oddly enough, they avoid smoking for the very reason I avoid mountains. It is too risky.

I wonder how long it will be before the health and safety nuts start to go after the mountain climbers. They don't climb mountains or smoke cigarettes because the risk is far outweighed by any conceivable benefit. They want to avoid all risk, and you cannot speak to them of the rush you get on top of the mountain, or the rush you get from that first cigarette with your morning coffee. Not content to avoid risk themselves, they insist that everybody else think and act as they do.

This is what is particularly distressing about the lawsuits against the tobacco companies seeking, supposedly, to have the tobacco companies pay for the social costs of their products. The plaintiffs argued that since smoking causes various health problems, the companies that sell the products by which people incur these diseases ought to pay for the cost of treating these diseases. At first glance, this seems to make a lot of sense and is even quite just, but it is only a matter of time before this principle of law that was applied in the tobacco cases will be applied to every other product.

Mountain climbing, like smoking, entails certain social costs. Climbers fall to their deaths, and their minor dependents get Social Security benefits. Climbers break legs and heads, and the cost of treating these injuries increases health-care premiums for us all. Will the makers of pitons, rope, and ice axes become responsible for the medical and social costs of mountain climbing?

What a field day for lawyers! Under products liability law, they can seek to recover large sums for products that are defective. Skis, motorcycles, and woodworking tools all entail certain social costs even when used as intended. What a boon to the law business it will be to recover for products that are not defective.

Smoking is different, it is argued. Smoking is addictive, but surely the impulse to have a cigarette is no more addictive than the impulse that would compel a woman to leave her family, to travel halfway around the world, to find death on the side of a mountain. Smoking deaths are entirely preventable, but only if we prevent smoking. Mountain climbing deaths are just as preventable. We could prevent all mountain climbing deaths by banning mountain climbing.

I can imagine the opening statement of the plaintiff's lawyer in the jury trial against Big Rope, the rope and piton manufacturers. He would talk about how these companies were only interested in profits. Big Rope suppressed studies that showed people died from falling off mountains, and other studies that proved the ignorant, gullible climbers were unaware of this hazard. Even worse, Big Rope went after teenagers by encouraging rock climbing in summer camps and building rock walls in gymnasiums. The lawyer will note that Big Rope makes it a point to place advertising for their products where impressionable teenagers can see them, like *Boys' Life*. "Most climbers," the lawyer will say looking the jury square in the eye, "begin as teenagers, and Big Rope cynically recruits them as replacements because their consumer base of old climbers falls off."

The suits against the tobacco companies were brought by people who didn't smoke and didn't want others to either. Much as I am disinclined to climb mountains, I feel no need to stop the people who do. I think it would be a hoot, however, to be the plaintiff's lawyer in the Big Rope case.

Life is not without risk, and enjoying life is an even riskier proposition. Still, the world seems full of those who would prohibit others from undertaking risks or enjoying life. Much as they are afraid of death, they are afraid of life. They want to live to a ripe old age, and I wish them well, but the thought of mindlessly wandering the halls of some nursing home is not that attractive. That expedition to K2 made their choice, and died a preventable death much as smokers choose preventable deaths.

In a free society, the right to choose your own risk is more important than health, or even life itself.

THE SURGEON GENERAL HAS DETERMINED THAT THIS KIND OF THING IS HAZARDOUS TO YOUR HEALTH.

CHAPTER 15

Religion

In high school, our English teacher told us about a small sect who believed that Shakespeare was divinely inspired and that the works of Shakespeare were the word of God. The English teacher, a Catholic priest no less, said that while he did not agree with these heretical views, he would concede that Shakespeare was much better reading than, say, Matthew or Nahum.

I often think of this sect when considering the positions of the various religious fundamentalists, both Christian and Muslim. Both insist on a literal reading and interpretation of sacred script. I wonder why fundamentalists have such a poor opinion of God as a writer. Literal writing is very easy and almost anyone can do it. Look at me! But a writer who can use metaphors, similes, and analogies creates subtleties and nuances that more accurately describe the complex and enigmatic moral problems we face. God says we should do good to one another, and we should, but writers like Hawthorne ask, Is making someone wear a scarlet A doing good? Thou shalt not kill, but in all honesty it sometimes appears necessary, or even moral, to drop a laser-guided bomb on somebody.

There is a sort of blasphemous underpinning to religious fundamentalism that seeks to define God, that is *definire*, to set limits, on the deity who is *a priori* unlimited. Man is created in the image of God, but literalist people turn this upside down by arguing that since I am a literalist, God must also be a literalist. In effect, they create God in their own image.

The religious fundamentalists have a counterpart in the nonreligious fundamentalists on the left, which brings us back to Shakespeare. Let us suppose a judge hangs on the wall of his courtroom these lines from *Measure for Measure*, act 2 scene 1: "Tis one thing to be tempted, Escalus, tis another thing to fall. I do not deny the jury passing on the prisoner's life may, in the sworn twelve, have a thief or two guiltier than him they try."

Courts have a hard enough time getting jurors as it is so it will never happen, but lets suppose it did. One of those offended by the divine words of Shakespeare would file for an injunction. At trial the plaintiff would offer testimony from the bishop of this Shakespearean sect that the words of Shakespeare are the word of God, and demand the quote be taken down as promoting religion. In the judge's opinion, denying the injunction, he says something to the effect that just because some people believe Shakespeare is divine script doesn't make quoting him a religious exercise. Shakespeare is a well-known writer and his works and words are an integral part of our historical and literary tradition. The mere fact that a few people regard it as an expression of religious sentiment cannot be a basis for suppression.

Now let's suppose that a judge gets sued in federal court for hanging a copy of the Ten Commandments from the book of Exodus in the Bible. The only thing the court can know for sure about the Bible is that it was written a long time ago and that, like Shakespeare, it is an integral part of our historical and literary tradition. When these cases go to court, the federal courts invariably find that posting the Ten Commandments is the establishment of religion and should be suppressed.

So what's the difference between Shakespeare and Exodus? Apparently since a whole bunch of people believe that the Bible is the word of God, and only few believe in Shakespeare, one is establishing religion and the other is not. Suppression is based not on religious belief, but the majority status of the believers. And this is what passes for freedom of religion today.

I often thought back in the days when I was running for office that I would hang the Ten Commandments in my courtroom so that I would get sued and score a lot of points with the religious conservatives, who tended not to vote for me. I never did though, because I was afraid that when I was called to testify and put under oath, I would have to give an answer like this: "I am not religious at all. I hung the Ten Commandments for purely political reasons because I have a lot of religious zealots in my district." Such candor would have been counterproductive, and it would leave federal court in a dilemma. While you cannot hang the Ten Commandments for religious reasons, can you hang them for political reasons?

There are a lot who post the Ten Commandments solely to get sued, ordered to remove them, and re-elected. Whenever this happens, invariably some nonreligious fundamentalist takes the bait and gets a court order to have the Ten Commandments taken down. This is, the federal courts have ruled establishment of religion because a lot of people believe the Bible is the word of God.

There is a trend in the law, a bad trend, to argue about religious matters in terms of the right of free expression rather than in terms of freedom of religion. For example, there have been several cases where street preachers who follow the biblical mandate to go into streets and preach to all people are given protection from laws prohibiting such conduct on the grounds that people have the right to speak publicly, regardless of whether this speech has a religious meaning or not. These cases do not protect the religious right to do so.

There was a guy who used to preach in front of the court house where I worked, right under the windows in my office. He had a powerful voice, but he wore out after about twenty-five minutes of stentorian cries about hellfire, the whores of Babylon, and the Sodomites. Since it was hard to get any work done my clerks and I would often look down on him and discuss the theological implications of what he was saying. Once when he was going on about the Sodomites, we deliberated on the fact that when God destroyed the Sodomites for their sodomy, He also destroyed Gomorrah. We pondered the question, What would gomorrahy be, and would we like it?

Another time we discussed his rights, and all of the clerks took a free speech position; *i.e.*, that he had the right of free expression to be a pain in the ass and we had a duty to put up with it. I took a religious freedom stance. This guy was not engaging in speech, he was practicing his religion, and we had a similar duty to put up with that.

Several recent United States Supreme Court decisions have ruled that prayers before a high school commencement or football game are the establishment of religion. Many commentators have applauded the decision saying that religion is a private thing. Perhaps. But a lot of religious practice is done in a most public way.

I am hardly an expert on religious practice but I have seen TV footage of Shiite Muslims flagellating themselves on public streets. I saw a huge crowd of Hindus engaging in a ritual near Kuala Lumpur. Closer to home, I witnessed a statue of the Madonna being paraded by Catholics through Little Italy as was done in the movie *The Godfather, Part II*. I have seen fundamentalist revivalists on parade also. To be sure, much religious practice is very private. The Jews, no doubt as a result of centuries of repression, tend to avoid public displays and I have never seen an Episcopalian or Unitarian, *per quod*, doing anything in the streets.

However, starting things out with a prayer has a long tradition in the U.S. This tradition is reflected by Congress opening with a prayer from its chaplain and the blessing invoked by the Supreme Court at its opening. They always say a prayer at a new president's inauguration.

I have attended lots of meetings and dinners that began with an invocation by a local clergyman. At political meetings, you can get a good idea about the demographic makeup of the district when a white rabbi does the innovation and a black AME minister gives the benediction. As these public prayers were being said, the various nonbelievers maintained a respectful silence not so much out of respect for the deity being invoked, but out of deference for the beliefs of others. To say that one is being forced to pray as the crowd around you asks God's blessing is like saying that one is being forced to accept the main speaker's position on gun control or Social Security. I have heard a lot of prayers and a lot of drivel. In such cases, one can keep quiet and think and do as one wants.

This is where the problem with the courts comes in. While there may be genuine divergence of opinion on whether religious practice is an entirely private matter, once the Supreme Court, or any court for that matter, decides an issue like this it is, in effect, deciding the nature and extent of acceptable religious practice. In a free society, courts should not have that kind of power. To be sure, there are religious excesses such as mandated school prayer where the school kids were ordered by the school board to stand up each morning and to pray. Clearly, this is forced prayer. Creationism is dogma, not science.

The problem with religious decisions is that they will come back to haunt us. This is particularly true of decisions that enjoin a certain religious practice or habit. Where the government—and the courts are just a branch of the government—suppresses some kind of religious activity, it adds a bit more weight to the idea that the government can regulate religion for whatever reasons that seem compelling at the time.

Establishment of religion has never been a problem. England and Saudi Arabia both have established religions, but England long ago abandoned the suppression of non-established religious practice. The Jews in Spain lived for centuries under Islamic Moorish rule, but after the Christian *reconquista* it was not the establishment of the Catholic Church that caused them harm, it was the Inquisition.

Historically, religious majorities were almost never suppressed; it was almost always the minorities. We have a long tradition that holds that the majority must tolerate the minority. Now we have come full circle. We would not accept a case where a person holding majority religious views seeks to suppress some minority religious practice because he is offended by it, but we will allow suppression of majority practice if some minority is offended.

Simply put, the duty of religious tolerance is being eroded. We should ask, Does not the religious minority have a duty of tolerance also?

If one holds a minority religious belief, one should be most concerned about suppression. If a minority person is really concerned about freedom of religion, then one would expect that suppression of any religious practice would give him pause. To argue that I don't have to tolerate this because I don't believe in it, and to go to court to enforce my will, expands the class of things that can be suppressed. Even worse, it extends the line of cases that stand as precedent for the proposition that some kinds of religious activity can be banned.

The first amendment to the Constitution says that Congress shall pass no law establishing any religion or prohibiting the free exercise thereof. The first amendment doesn't say anything about the courts, and that's a problem. Every time they decide one of these religion cases, it is the judicial branch of government deciding what is acceptable religious practice. Where is that wall of separation between church and state?

CHAPTER 16

The Law

Lawyers

I suppose I should say a word or two about what swine
lawyers are, but frankly they are such an easy target,
so let me just say this. If you people were kind and decent
to each other, we lawyers would all be out of work.

Demeaning Jobs

I often hear people, particularly young people, complain
about having no employment opportunity except for
"some demeaning job." I wonder at this because they
always go on to characterize it as "some demeaning job like
flipping burgers or mopping floors." Whatever example
they use, almost invariably I have done that kind of work
while working my way through college and law school.

I used to be the American Dream. As one of eight children of immigrant parents, I followed the traditional

American Dream career path—work a semester, school a semester, and so on—until twelve years later I graduated from law school and went into politics. Times change, they say, and the American Dream no longer exists and I have become, I suppose, a vestigial Powerful White Male. The unfortunate thing about this talk about demeaning jobs is that it gives young people the impression that once you become a Powerful White Male, the demeaning work stops. Unfortunately, not.

I wanted to be a lawyer because the law is the most basic principle on which society rests. All the other careers and disciplines—science, medicine, business, art rely on the stability and continuity that the legal system provides. No society can survive unless its legal system meets the people's reasonable expectation of justice, and no society can prosper unless the law promotes and protects individual freedom. In American society, the concepts of justice and freedom are often defined by the United States Supreme Court. Judges on the lower courts, such as myself, are bound to follow the law as set by the highest court. Janitor or judge, your job is to do what the higher-ups tell you has to be done. This is where it gets demeaning.

As a janitor, I was not demeaned when told to do something like wash windows, perhaps because I had no strong feeling about the task. I do, however, have very strong feelings about what is just and what is right. As a judge, I feel demeaned by some of the things the U.S. Supreme Court would have me do.

For example, in *Colorado v. Connelly*, a man approached

a policeman in Denver and said the voice of God had told him to fly from Boston to Denver to confess to a murder he had committed there the year before. The Colorado Supreme Court refused to admit the confession on the grounds that he was delusional and the confession was neither voluntary or reliable. The U.S. Supreme Court reversed, although Justices Brennan and Marshall, in dissenting, suggested that perhaps we should not accept the confession of a madman.

For over a thousand years, English-speaking people had the right to travel the highways freely, but the Court has approved random DUI roadblocks and identity checks like in some World War II movie about the Nazis. They have abrogated the right of one spouse to not testify against the other, merely a four-hundred-year-old right, on the grounds that it was outdated, as if married couples today no longer need to be able to communicate confidentially. And aside from any Constitutional implication, if a spouse really wants to testify against the other spouse, how biased and unreliable is that testimony likely to be?

In *Herrera*, a death penalty case, the defendant sought habeas relief on the grounds that there was substantial evidence that he was innocent, that they had in fact convicted the wrong guy, but the court said that "actual innocence" does not raise a constitutional question. Our Supreme court said that habeas corpus is not available to correct errors of fact, but only ."... to insure that individuals are not imprisoned in violation of the Constitution."

I had always assumed that the courts had the constitutional duty to intervene on behalf of the innocent, and that decision brought me back to my janitorial days. There were a few, even then, who thought some work beneath them, the "we don't do windows" crowd. I did not like having to work with those who would draw a paycheck and not do the work. I still feel that way. But here I am, linked in the legal system to those same kind of slackers. Like those slacker janitors, some of the justices on the U. S. Supreme Court are satisfied to make a pass with the constitutional mop, but don't care if the floor is really clean or if the result is really just.

Most frustrating is that they would have me, as a lower court judge, engage in this same sloppy practice. They would have me affirm the confessions of lunatics, ignore traditional rights and duties, and erase that clear line which, over the centuries, has been carefully drawn between personal freedom and limited government action. They would have me send a man to his death and not be concerned whether he is "actually innocent."

It has been a long time since I mopped floors, but as I remember it, janitors had more integrity then, and I regard this "we don't do windows" attitude as a sad devolution in standards. I am no longer a janitor, but instead have a prestigious, statusy job that many young people think they might like to have some day. The unfortunate truth, however, is that I now sit in my office and read the Supreme Court opinions that say they don't do innocence and think to myself, "Boy, this is really demeaning work."

The Death Penalty

The death penalty as an issue is a bit peculiar because while you can usually predict a person's position on any issue based on whether he is a liberal or a conservative, when it comes to the death penalty party line discipline falls apart. For example, a conservative friend of mind told me he was against the death penalty. How conservative was he? Well, he was enough of a conservative to be named by President Reagan to the federal bench.

He was against the death penalty because study after study had shown that it had no deterrent effect and he felt it was unconstitutional to impose any penalty that had no deterrent effect. During his Senate confirmation hearings, no one asked him about his stand on the death penalty. It is hard to imagine a Democratic nominee getting a pass on that one.

For myself, a liberal, I am opposed to the death penalty but only on very illiberal, nonmoral grounds. My objection is entirely practical. I have been a judge for over twenty-five years and I have seen how the system works.

We do the best we can but the unfortunate truth is that the law is not very good in dealing with emotional issues. When we decide what the contract says, or where the property line is, we are usually right on the money. When we get into emotional issues like divorce and custody, the testimony from the witnesses is likewise emotional, thus less probative and compelling, and so the decisions reflect that lack of precision. When the jury hears the young widow testify about how her husband was working the night shift at the 7-Eleven so he could finish college and how he was shot by some punk in an unprovoked attack, it is almost all emotion.

If you read the papers, you will see that the courts almost never get it right. We give custody to the wrong parent, we award enormous sums of money to people with spurious claims, and we let criminals walk free on technicalities. In spite of all this, Americans are convinced that when the courts sentence a man to death they are absolutely right. And, in most cases, they are, but you wouldn't want to bet your life on it. You don't want to bet somebody else's life, either.

Drugs

A while ago in the morning paper there was a picture of
the attorney general, who was announcing the arrest of
sixty-four people involved in heroin smuggling and distri-
bution. I was mighty pleased to read about this bust. Since
these people have been arrested, there will be no more
heroin coming into the country and the people who are
addicted to it will not be able to get any. Since the addicts
will not able to get any heroin, they will no doubt give up
the habit, and our drug problems will be over with. Ta da!

I felt good all day about this, but unfortunately, I stayed
up to watch *The French Connection* on TV. It is a really
good movie, and although it was made in 1971, it still is has
a contemporary theme. Two cops, Gene Hackman and Roy
Scheider, rush about New York behaving like a couple of
hoodlums threatening and assaulting people and in general violating all sorts of laws and everyone's civil rights.

After about two hours of this official thuggery, they
seize sixty kilos of heroin secreted in the rocker panels of
a Lincoln, but the drug kingpin gets away.

This movie could be made today, except that no audi-
ence would believe that the smugglers would go to all that
trouble more a mere sixty kilos—only 132 pounds. If they
do a remake, it would have to be at least a ton, but other
than that everything in the war on drugs is the same as it
was twenty-five years ago. Drugs are widely available, the
cops are violating everyone's civil rights, and the guys who

profit most from all this, except for occasionally being murdered by a competitor, never seem to suffer much. Does anyone really think busting some drug dealers will do anything at all except change the faces of who makes the money?

So why do we ban drugs? Surely not for your benefit, and surely not for mine. If drugs were legal, you and I would eschew them, but there are some people who are not fit to care for themselves. If we didn't ban drugs, we would have people selling drugs on street corners and high school kids smoking pot at parties and college kids popping pills at raves, not like today.

The most remarkable thing about the drug laws is the conservatives' complete abandonment of their principles. Markets are efficient. Government is not. If this be true, and conservatives insist that it is, then the solution to the drug problem must be a market solution.

The market solution to drugs is not to just legalize them, but to have a nonmarket in drugs; *i.e.*, the government. Instead of having the government trying to suppress drugs, we will have the government trying to sell drugs. We would abolish the DEA, a remarkably unsuccessful agency, and replace it with the Bureau of Dope. The Drug Tsar would be gone and replaced with the Pot Potentate, or his Meth Majesty, or maybe even His Heroin Highness.

This would be a wonderful solution since it would appeal to the liberals by not only creating a new agency but a new source of revenue. It would appeal to the conservatives by getting the government off people's backs and would put to the test their idea that governments are always inefficient.

Gun Control

The debate over gun control seems to have one curious aspect. Gun control appears to be an attempt by a group of unarmed people to force their political will on another group of very well-armed people. This hardly ever, almost never, happens—a point made by Joe Stalin when he asked Roosevelt and Churchill, "How many divisions does the Pope have?"

Are the gun control people against the use of force? Not at all. The gun control people are all in favor of *some* people having guns, and using them, but only the right ones. That's what this whole debate is about. Who are the right people?

In the minds of the gun control people, anybody who wants to own or carry a gun is, *ipso facto*, one of the wrong people. Gun owners are invariably portrayed as borderline lunatics who will shoot at anything. If you would understand the absolutist intransigence of many gun owners to any sort of reasonable regulation, you should look to how they are usually characterized. Their reaction is not all that paranoiac.

I am an opponent of most gun control laws for several reasons—some grammatical. I paid attention in seventh-grade English class. There were forty-seven kids in my class and one nun, Sister Anselma. (There is a lot of talk nowadays about smaller classes being better, but a good teacher makes class size almost irrelevant.) In that class I learned what an independent clause is, what a dependent clause is, and the difference between a restrictive and nonrestrictive subordinate clause.

Look at the second amendment. It reads:

> *A well regulated militia, (comma)*
> *being necessary to the security of a free state, (comma)*
> *the right of the people to keep and bear arms, (comma)*
> *shall not be infringed. (period)*

The whole of the gun control debate comes down to an argument over which is the dependent and which is the inde pendent clause in that sentence. Had they written:

> *A well regulated militia*
> *is necessary to the security of a free state. (period)*
> *The right of the people to keep and bear arms*
> *shall not be infringed. (period)*

there would be no such debate.

In his classic, *The Elements of Style*, E. B. White suggests that writers use periods and not use commas. The second amendment to the constitution is a good example of why White, powerful white male that he was and dead white male that he now is, suggests this.

Being a judge, I have had the occasional death threat, but none that I regarded so seriously as to require me to start packing heat. Nor can I imagine a situation where, like some judges, I would sit on the bench with a gun under my robe. My position on gun control is based on what I learned from Sister Anselma in seventh-grade English. Thus, I must conclude, for reasons of grammar, that every American has a constitutional right to own and carry a gun.

I am also opposed to gun control for historical reasons. Our founding fathers were a bunch of rebels—gun-toting rebels. The whole rebellion began with a fight over the guns and ammunition stored at the arsenal at Concord. These dead white males were a bunch of guys who said in their Declaration of Independence, ". . .it is their right, it is their duty . . ." to throw off despotic governments. You don't hear much about duties any more, but people who feel they have a duty to overthrow the government do not give up their guns.

Many of them, like Washington, had some experience with fighting Indians. At the time the constitution was being drafted the westward expansion over the Appalachians was causing more clashes with the Indians, and virtually every man at the constitutional convention could remember the brutal Indian raids during the French and Indian War and Pontiac's raids.

But it was not only the Indians. In the western reaches of some states there was no sort of police protection. Most of the inhabitants of the West were peaceful farmers, but there were a lot criminals and freebooters who went West to escape the law in the east. If you lived more than fifty or a hundred miles from the Atlantic, you needed and owned a gun.

The second amendment was just that—an amendment, a thing added on to improve the original. If the second amendment was intended only to provide for a state's right to have a militia, and not intended to guarantee an individual's right to bear arms, who would have voted for it?

Not the New England States. They had started a war with Great Britain, one of the most powerful nations on the face of the earth, in order to protect their right to keep the guns and ammunition stored at the arsenal at Concord. Surely not the Southern slave-holding states. The Constitution, as originally enacted, provided for the ownerships of slaves. Slavery is a brutal business so if you are going to own slaves, you probably ought to also own a gun. Certainly not the Westerners, living as they did close the Indians and always in danger from the freebooter.

But what about militia? There must have been some reason in the drafters' minds for including that word in the sentence. The word "militia" in the eighteenth century meant an armed citizenry, and was the direct opposite of a standing army. The buggaboo of eighteenth-century peaceniks was the standing army—sort of the weapon of mass destruction of its day. In 1788 they felt that if you have a standing army, somebody would be inclined to use it, and the only safe thing was to have a militia.

Thus, I must conclude, for reasons of history, that every American has a constitutional right to own and carry a gun.

There is a bit of the Luddite in the gun control people's attitude—the idea that if we ban the tool, we will eliminate the evils the tool causes. I was in the Soviet Union on one of those meet-the-other-country's-judges tours and learned that the most common weapon used in Russian homicides was the good old-fashioned ax. Most Russians who live outside the cities heat with wood, and the ax is a common household implement. When the urge to murder your spouse comes upon you, as it does in most marriages, you either stifle it or resort to what's handy. In low-tech Russia, it is the wood ax. In the high-tech USA, it is often a gun.

In truth, there are an awful lot of gun deaths in this country and this is the strongest point for the advocates of gun control. Gun homicides here in the United States is about forty-two persons per year per 100,000 population. That is pretty high. By comparison, in England is it about 6.2 and 5.2 in Switzerland.

That's shocking to some people, but I was shocked, though, by a series of articles that appeared in the *Cleveland Plain Dealer* a few years ago, written by an associate editor, Philip Morris. The substance of Morris's article was that the exceedingly high gun homicide rate in the U.S. was skewed by the fact that most of the homicides were of young black men between the ages of sixteen and twenty-five killing other young black men of the same age. For that demographic, the gun homicide rate was above fifty. If you deleted the black age sixteen to twenty-five deaths, the gun homicide rate for the U.S. was about 5.6, lower than England, and almost as low as peaceful

Switzerland. The point that Morris wanted to make was that drugs and gangs fighting over drug-dealing market share were taking an extraordinary toll on young black men.

If you are in favor of gun control, reread the section in this chapter about decriminalizing drug use.

CHAPTER 17

Conclusion

Vice

During the Monica Lewinski affair the newspapers and TV were full of commentary about the decline of all the standards in America. William Bennett wrote a book, *The Book of Virtues*, decrying our lack of virtue. Even today one can read regularly about how we are not as good as we used to be.

Have we lost our sense of values? I think not, and indeed the uproar over Lewinsky demonstrated that we have lip-service values and real values. Lip-service values encompass such things as honesty and marital fidelity. The Republicans seized on this in their attempt to pillory Clinton and could not understand why the country did not share their sense of outrage. This is not to say that the country was not outraged, but the people were upset over other matters, which demonstrate what they really value.

Americans value friendship and condemn false friends.

Virtually every one of those caught up in this melodramatic soap opera—Bill, Monica, Hillary, Kenneth, Newt, and Orrin—was castigated by some and defended by others. Except Linda Tripp. She was roundly condemned by all. She betrayed her friend. She ratted Monica out. Even the Clinton haters who were quite willing to avail themselves of the opportunity she presented to get him had little good to say on her behalf. Perhaps some of America's traditional values have gone by the boards, but the loathing and contempt we have for betrayal is as strong as ever.

Monicagate also demonstrated another important American value—discretion. All the while this was going on, Newt Gingrich was having an affair, but he was discrete about it so it was okay. Clinton's failure, and one for which he was denounced by even his most ardent supporters, was his absolute lack of discretion. He was having a young girl give him blow jobs, conduct which in the minds of half the population (men) is not all that disreputable. After all, people are always talking about the president being the most powerful man in the world, and one of the defining qualities of being the most powerful man is to get a blow job when you want it.

But he was doing it in his office, in the same house where his wife lived. He was doing it a way almost certain to ensure that it would become public knowledge, which would embarrass his wife and daughter. Discretion is an American value.

So is privacy. Discretion is a value because we do not wish to be put into a position where we intrude on someone else's privacy, and when one is indiscrete, we must deal with facts we would rather not know about. We condemn infidelity not by stoning the adulterer, but by recognizing it as a danger to any marriage and a problem for those in that marriage to work out. But it is their problem, and a private problem, and unless and until one of them comes to you and wants to talk about it, it's none of your business.

Kenneth Starr, the media, and the Republican Congress all violated the rule against invading one's privacy. The American public reacted much the same way a court does when the police conduct an illegal search of a private home—they suppressed the evidence. The right to privacy is an American value, one so ingrained in the American psyche that we are even willing to extend it to our president.

Hypocrisy still offends most Americans and Clinton's hypocrisy would have been enough to earn him the disapprobation he deserved had it not been overwhelmed by the hypocrisy of his detractors. Every few weeks some Republican congressman would take the floor and confess about some affair, and the congressional leadership would follow up by saying that they were not going after Clinton for the sex but because of perjury. Perjury? Lying about sex is not perjury, and when one considers the duty to be discrete, it is mandatory.

Have we lost our sense of values? No, not at all. We have lost our sense of vice. Throughout history we have condemned vice, meaning other people's vices, but we have never really tried to stop people from exercising their God-given right to sin. Prohibition was a deviation from that sensible policy and we learned our lesson there. Or did we?

People engage in conduct that for others is meaningless, unenjoyable, or possibly even harmful. For some people the urge to engage in that conduct is compulsive, and we describe that as a vice. For others, the urge to keep other people from harm, to save them from their vices, is irresistible. They used to be in a minority. The old hippie slogan, "you do your thing and I'll do mine," was a rule of thumb that we all followed.

Some of us are homosexual, and some are religious fundamentalists. The homosexuals condemn the fundamentalists for their narrowmindedness, and in return fundamentalists decry their sinful ways. For most of us, though, it really doesn't matter all that much, and we view both as a kind of aberrant and excessive lifestyle—a vice, if you will. Both sides, however, are not content to leave us alone, and insist that we condemn what they regard as vice.

I am not religious, but some people find religion helps make some sense out of this difficult thing called life. I am not a homosexual, but everyone needs a little love and comfort in his life. For me, religion and homosexuality are both vices, but if saying a prayer helps relieve some of the stress of life, or if a man can only find the love he needs in the arms of another man, so be it. When one man finds God and another man finds man, they are both better off for it, and so are we as a society.

I have in this book given you my list of vices—mathematics, feminism, mountain climbing, fitness, eating right, and so on. I do not engage in any of these aberrant behaviors, but I tolerate them all.

That's the secret of the Jelly Donut Diet. Enjoy what you like: it is a virtue. Avoid what you don't like; it is a vice. But above all else, let others have their vices, too.